THE GIFT OF GOODBYE

A story for kids of all ages who love someone with Alzheimer's Disease

LOUISE CYPRESS

Copyright 2018 by Louise Cypress

All rights reserved. No part of this book may be reproduced, stored in a retrieved system, or transmitted, in any form or by any means, electronic, mechanical, recording or otherwise, without the prior written permission of the publisher, except in the case of a reviewer, who may quote brief passages in a review to print in a magazine, newspaper or blog post.

Cover design by James from GoOnWrite.com

For my Grandma Darlene

1
IT ALL STARTED AT THE OLIVE GARDEN

CALEB ADLER wasn't normally a butthead. He was more like a sixth grade bulldog. Caleb would do anything to protect his family, even bite. Of course, Caleb never actually bit someone—not since preschool at least—but he would if he had to.

"Did I order this?" asked Caleb's grandma as they sat at the Olive Garden.

"Yes, Grams. You did," Caleb answered.

Grams stared at her pasta. "What is it, Walter?"

"It's spaghetti, Mom. Your favorite." Caleb's father looked away. It was hard for Mr. Adler to acknowledge how far Grams's memory had slipped.

"Yum," said Caleb's twin brother Tyler. "Look at all that cheese."

Caleb stared at his own plate of lasagna and drooled.

But he waited for everyone to be served, like Grams had taught him.

The waiter put down the last dish and Grams took a bite. "You're right!" she said brightly. "This is delicious. Only, I need to visit the ladies' room."

What if she gets lost? Caleb thought. Too bad his mom and sister weren't there.

"I'll go with you," said Mr. Adler.

"No, I'll go," offered Caleb. "No biggie." He climbed out of the booth and followed.

When they got to the restrooms Caleb sent Grams into the women's by herself. Then he waited. And waited. And waited. Finally he saw another lady come by, a mom with a baby. "Um... Excuse me." Caleb dug his toe into the carpet. "My grandma's in there and she has Alzheimer's. Could you please check on her?"

"Sure," the mom said, as the baby yanked on her earring.

At that exact moment Emma Silver came out of the restroom. "Tyler?" Emma asked, guessing the wrong twin.

"No, Caleb."

"Oh, my gosh!" Emma laughed. "You won't believe it! There's an old lady at the sink with her pants down."

"That's my grandma," said Caleb, trying not to spit the words out. Emma flinched. Caleb pushed past Emma into the women's restroom. His adrenaline pumped so fast, he wasn't even embarrassed.

Grams stood in front of the mirror with her pants pooled around her ankles. Toilet paper fluttered from her hand. "Walter?" Grams asked Caleb. "Where did Sonia go?"

"Who's Sonia?" Caleb asked. He tried not to look at his grandma's underwear. He tried not to remember the hundreds of times—no, the thousands of times—Grams took *him* to the bathroom when he was little. Now the tables were turned and it really sucked. "It'll be okay, Grams," said Caleb. But it wasn't okay. Caleb was crying, and he wasn't the type of boy who cried. *I should have let Dad take Grams to the restroom,* Caleb thought. *This is too hard!*

Luckily, the mom with the baby came back. She took one look and shoved her macaroni-covered infant into Caleb's arms. "Hold him while I help your grandmother." Then she escorted Grams into the stall.

It was the longest three minutes of Caleb's life. The baby looked at him and giggled, which made Caleb think about Emma, laughing at Grams. He felt like he'd been punched in the gut.

It was pain that wouldn't go away. It was still there during the car ride home, and the next morning at breakfast. Caleb didn't want to tell anyone—especially Tyler—what happened to Grams in the restroom. It was too humiliating for an eleven-year-old to bear. His brother would probably freak out. Or worse—throw up. Tyler always blew chunks when he was upset. Their mom said Tyler had a nervous disposition.

Caleb was a lot tougher. But that didn't stop the torment inside him from building up bigger and bigger until it was lunchtime at school in the stinky cafeteria. When Caleb saw Emma, he finally snapped.

SYDNEY TAYLOR watched Emma's fingers trace the air and knew her best friend was in trouble. That's what Emma did when she tried to remember a number. Sydney wanted to whisper the answer to Emma. *Forty-six, twenty-two.* But she couldn't. They were right in the middle of the lunch line and everyone stared.

"Your pin code?" the cafeteria worker asked, but Emma's blue eyes were wide and blank.

"What's the matter, Airhead?" Caleb used Emma's terrible nickname. "Are you too dumb to buy lunch?" His twin brother Tyler stood there too, holding his plate of tacos.

"Leave her alone, Caleb!" Sydney shook back her pink-tipped hair and bunched up her fists.

Emma wasn't dumb. She had dyslexia—a big difference. But Sydney knew that Emma wouldn't be able to remember her lunch code with all the pressure. Caleb's friend Drake snorted with laughter.

Emma stumbled with her tray and French fries went flying. "Forget it," Emma said. She abandoned her food on the floor and walked away.

When Sydney bent down to clean things up, Caleb and his friends stepped over her like she was a roadblock. Everyone but Tyler. He tried to help, but Sydney shrugged him off.

Sydney tracked down Emma to where she was slumped behind the vending machine next to the band room. She handed Emma a chocolate milk and sat down too. "I knew you'd be here," said Sydney.

Emma wiped back tears and gouged the carton with her straw. "You knew I'd hide?"

"And worry too much. Does it matter what Caleb thinks?"

Emma sucked up air through her nose, fighting back the snot. "It's not that." Then Emma cried so hard she couldn't stop. "Why does everything have to be so hard for me? Even things that are supposed to be easy, like saying my lunch code?"

"Lunch codes are silly. Don't worry about them. You're still one of the smartest people I know."

"If I'm so smart, why does the whole sixth grade think I'm stupid?"

Sydney rolled her eyes. "Don't exaggerate."

"But the boys—"

"—are losers. Who cares what they think?" Sydney adjusted the netting on her skirt. It was black ruffled tulle and looked absolutely perfect with her motorcycle boots and skull shirt.

Emma hugged her knees tight. "I don't care about them, but I wish Caleb didn't think I was horrible."

Sydney put her arms around Emma's back, careful to make sure that the ink from the doodles on her wrist didn't rub off on Emma's sweater. "Why would he think you're horrible?"

Emma shuddered. "Never mind."

Sydney leaned her head against Emma's shoulder. She hated Caleb for making Emma cry. Sydney didn't have any control over the miserable things that happened in her own life—like her dad dying—but she was determined to protect her best friend.

"Don't worry," Sydney told Emma. "I'll make Caleb pay. He'll never call you a name again."

EMMA SILVER knew everyone at Whitman Elementary called her "Airhead" behind her back. Caleb was just bold enough to say it to her face. At school, the only time Emma felt safe was when she had pull-out with Miss Klimey, the special ed teacher.

Emma's life was like this, in the morning she went to Miss Klimey for specialized instruction in reading and math, then the rest of the day Emma was mainstreamed with the other students in Mr. Baker's regular-ed class. Emma hated the word "mainstreamed." It made her feel like a salmon swimming upstream in the Snohomish River. But unlike a fish swimming towards its death, Emma had a fighting chance for survival because Miss Klimey knew there were a billion ways to learn besides reading a textbook. The day after her lunch line humiliation, Miss Klimey had Emma build her lunch code out of clay so she'd never forget it again: 4622.

Emma was coming out of the washroom where she'd cleaned clay off her hands when she ran into Tyler. Sweat popped up on Emma's forehead. She took a deep breath and dove into her apology. "Caleb, I'm sorry about the Olive Garden. I didn't realize she was your grandma. It was weird when she called me 'Sonia,' so I laughed. But that's no excuse."

Tyler pulled hair across his forehead, covering the scar he got during a particularly vicious foursquare match. Some people used that scar to tell Tyler and Caleb apart. But not Emma.

"I wish I go could go back in time and help your

grandma clean up instead of walking away," Emma said. "Can you forgive me?"

Tyler's coffee-colored eyes turned dark. He didn't say anything for a while, which made Emma jittery. Then he said, "I'll think about it." But right when Emma was about to walk back to Miss Klimey's room, Tyler said, "Hey, Emma. I'm sorry about yesterday. I shouldn't have said you were dumb."

Emma shrugged her shoulders like she wasn't still hurting. And then Emma said what she wished she could hear: "That's okay. I forgive you."

TYLER ADLER's emotional control was as strong as a wet paper napkin. If he was happy, he was loud. If he was angry, he raged. If something bothered him, Tyler said the same darn thing over and over again until the rest of his family went nuts. Sometimes Tyler's emotions got so big and messy that they made him feel sick to his stomach. If there was a math test at school, Tyler couldn't eat breakfast—not even if his mom bought donuts.

Tyler hated watching Caleb humiliate Emma at lunch. That's why Tyler pretended to be Caleb and apologized to Emma, although the twins didn't normally switch places without each other's permission. Tyler felt things deeply—especially bad things.

At the moment, Tyler was stuck in class while Mr. Baker lectured about ancient Egypt. Instead of discussing something cool like mummies or pyramids, Mr. Baker made social studies all about "summarize this" and "regurgitate that." It was a whole lot of barfing up barf. Mr. Baker's thick glasses and bulging stomach reminded Tyler of a slug.

Tyler tuned out and looked across the classroom. He saw Sydney over in the corner. Her hair was the whitest blonde Tyler had ever seen, and her head was bent so low that Tyler couldn't see her face until she looked up at him and glared. Right then a paper airplane hit him in the head. Sydney smiled wickedly. Tyler looked behind him, but he couldn't tell who'd sent it. The airplane had fancy script that read, "OPEN ME," so Tyler did.

Inside he found a cartoon of Caleb dressed in his soccer uniform and kicking a bottle of laxatives. Tyler knew it was Caleb and not himself because the letters C-A-L-E-B were spelled on the jersey. Poop shot out of Caleb's butt!

Tyler scanned the room again, trying to figure out where the plane came from, but it was impossible to tell. His whole body cringed. *Who's the jerk who drew this?*

2
POOPY PICTURES CAUSE PROBLEMS

SYDNEY had printed two hundred copies of that caricature and stayed up until midnight folding them into paper airplanes. This morning, Sydney scattered the airplanes all around the school.

Now it was lunch and Sydney and Emma sat at their cafeteria table. Emma's planner was spread out between them and she had her color-coded pens. Karen and Tiffany sat with them, mesmerized by the caricature of Caleb.

"Who do you think did that?" Karen held out the picture of Caleb. "It's soooo funny."

Tiffany leaned in for a closer look. "No idea, but it's the funniest cartoon I've ever seen."

Cartoon! It isn't a cartoon—it's a caricature, Sydney thought. But she stayed mum.

"Do you think Tyler drew it? He's the only person I know who can draw that well." It was hard to understand Karen because she had a fork-full of noodles in her mouth.

"Nah," Tiffany answered. "I found a bunch of them in the girls' bathroom. Plus, Tyler wouldn't do that to his own brother."

Sydney dipped a tater tot in ketchup. "Maybe this will make Caleb keep his mouth shut," she said casually. Emma looked at her sharply, and Sydney knew that Emma knew.

"Can I see it?" Emma asked. Karen handed the paper over and Emma put down her highlighter. "Look at the caption," Emma said. "Here. I'll read it." Her words came out slowly, but perfectly. "Poop… is… his… secret… super… power.'" Emma looked at her friends' faces. "Why aren't you laughing? That's hysterical!"

Karen and Tiffany were both holding their breath. Sydney was so nervous for Emma, reading something aloud, that she froze solid. But now that it was over, Sydney chuckled. "Yeah," said Sydney. "It doesn't matter how many times I hear it. It's still funny."

When the twins finally entered the cafeteria, the whole room went silent. Caleb and Tyler lifted up plastic sporks. "Crapeteria food?" Tyler said. "You have been warned!" Then Caleb added, "Stop being disgusting or risk the wrath of my butt!"

The roar in the room was so deafening that the floor vibrated. The Adler twins appeared cooler than ever. And Sydney knew, she just knew, everyone was laughing with Caleb, not at him. Sydney jammed another tater-tot into her mouth and the ketchup smeared like blood on her lips.

CALEB and Tyler geared up for soccer practice later that afternoon in the back of their dad's SUV. The whole car smelled like wet gym socks and Caleb's shin guards were itchy. "Wonderful Seattle sunshine," he grumbled, looking at the rain.

"Yeah, it's a regular flood," Tyler answered. "Hey, are you okay?"

"Why wouldn't I be?"

"Um... the picture."

"It was stupid. No big deal." Caleb tightened his cleats and resisted the urge to growl.

"Okay. Whatever. But I want you to know that I'm going to find out who did it." Tyler held up his hand and made a sign-language "c." It was the opening of their signature handshake.

Caleb smiled hard. He made a "t" in return. They were just doing the fist-bump when Drake knocked on the rear window. Caleb popped open the tailgate and the cold poured in.

"Come on, slackers! Practice in five minutes. My dad's redoing the starting line-up."

"We'll be there," Tyler said. Then he looked at Caleb. He didn't have to say one word for Caleb to know what was going on. Tyler was so nervous that he was going to hurl. Tyler was pretty good at soccer, but nowhere near as skilled as Caleb.

"You'll be fine," Caleb said. "You'll do great."

"'Course I will." But then Tyler clenched his stomach and turned green. "I just have to…" Tyler took off running for the bathroom at full speed.

With some sort of psychic twin thing, Caleb remembered that Tyler ate spaghetti for lunch. But when Caleb saw Tyler's team sweatshirt bunched up on the floor, he got an idea of how to help. Caleb slipped the hoodie with "T-Y-L-E-R" spelled out in big black letters over his head. *Double the power. Double the awesome,* he thought.

Twenty minutes later when the real Tyler finally came back from the bathroom, Drake's dad had made his decision. "Great hustle, Tyler!" he yelled across the field to Caleb.

"Thanks!" Caleb shouted back, waving.

EMMA knew right away it was Sydney who had drawn that cartoon about Caleb. Once when Emma was having a hard time in fourth grade, Sydney drew the history of Washington State for Emma on a long piece of butcher paper. Sydney made Lewis and Clark look like they were actually having a good time. Emma memorized the mural and aced the test.

Emma was really proud of Sydney's talent and grateful for her loyalty. So yesterday she texted Sydney a smiley face and wrote "Thx."

Of course, Emma couldn't think about Sydney's picture now because she was in Mr. Baker's classroom for her weekly check-in, supported by Miss Klimey. Mr. Baker was seated at his gigantic desk while Miss Klimey and Emma were stuck in the front row like they were in trouble.

"We have some serious issues to discuss." Mr. Baker talked straight to Miss Klimey, like Emma wasn't in the room. "Emma's a lovely girl, but I'm concerned about her grades. Succeeding in my class means reading a lot of books and turning in well-structured written assignments. That's a hard order for any sixth grader, especially one with Emma's… challenges."

Emma felt like she was pushed into the deep end. She couldn't catch her breath. But Miss Klimey was awesome. She pointed her finger at Mr. Baker like he was the one in trouble. "Emma is one of the brightest, hardest working students I know." Despite her frizzy hair and pleated corduroy trousers, Miss Klimey was the most beautiful woman in the world.

Mr. Baker cleared his throat and pulled out a file folder. "Maybe you should take a look at Emma's last assignment."

Miss Klimey didn't take the offered file. "I've already read Emma's report on the Sphinx of Giza," she said, her eyes steely. "I helped her proofread. There's not one mistake."

"Correct spelling isn't enough, Nancy. I'm concerned with complexity."

When Mr. Baker said that, Miss Klimey took the paper. She glanced down at the red ink marking up the page. Emma did too. Right in the corner was a big, fat "D."

SYDNEY was holed up in her closet with a Sharpie. She angled her lamp so that every last inch of closet was lit. It took her forever to clear enough space to work. Board games lay haphazardly on the bed.

Sydney wanted everyone to think she was only a doodler. If there was a pen nearby, watch out. But nobody had seen what she could really do except her brother Brian and Emma. Sydney figured the fewer people who knew about her the better. Once your so-called talents and abilities were known, everybody expected you to do stuff.

"What the heck are you up to?" Brian asked, coming into her room. He crouched down to look at Sydney's artwork. "Is that ivy?"

"Poison ivy," Sydney corrected. Then she looked at him pointedly. "So stay away."

But Brian didn't go away. Instead, he slid over some hangers so he could see what else she had drawn back there. "Skunks and a cactus? Why can't you draw rainbows and sunshine?"

"Because that would be dumb." It was a lame retort. Sydney made a note to buy the low-odor Sharpies because the fumes made her head ache. "Is Mom home yet?"

"Nah, George is picking her up from the yoga studio for a Saturday-night date."

"Figures." Sydney looked down at her hands. Ink bled onto her fingertips.

"So you're coming with me to the skate park," Brian said matter-of-factly. "Put down your anarchy pen and let's get moving."

"Fine!" Sydney made a big display of scowling, but the truth was, she really didn't mind. Brian was five years older than her and a super good brother. Even though they fought, Sydney knew, deep-down dark in the place where it counted, Brian was her shelter.

"We're leaving in ten. Try to wear something normal!" Brian shouted as he left.

Normal? Why would I want to be that? Sydney asked herself. Today she looked like an American-Girl-doll ninja. She had on a polka-dot dress and a skull-and-bones sweater.

Brian and Sydney rolled in silence on the way to the park. The cracks of the sidewalk made clickety-clack sounds under Sydney's scooter. It had finally stopped raining.

At the park, Sydney found a corner where she could sit and draw while Brian pretended like he didn't know her. But now and then she saw Brian look over to make sure she was okay.

Then something weird happened. Sydney gave Brian's rainbows and unicorns a try. She also filled the paper with fluffy-white clouds and a castle straight out of *Cinderella*. Pretty soon her scene looked like a fairy had thrown up. That's when, before Sydney could stop herself, she added an angel up in the corner. She gave him a crooked smile and a fleece jacket. Sydney put a mug of coffee in his hand and drew the keychain to his Prius hanging out of his pocket.

Sydney's nose started to drip.

"You drew that?" asked a voice behind her. "It's spectacular!" Sydney turned to see a high school girl with blonde hair. She bent over the sketchpad before Sydney could stop her.

"Um... yeah." Sydney wiped her eyes with her sleeve.

Now Brian was there too, flipping up his board. "Is my little sister awesome or what?"

"Impressive," the girl said, as she fluttered her eyelashes at Brian.

Brian turned deep red. "Ava Adler," he said. "I'd like you to meet Sydney."

There was that flash again of perfectly straight teeth. "Pleased to meet you," Ava said. "Do you know my brothers, Caleb and Tyler? They're probably your age."

Sydney smiled back, but inside she knew her day of doom was coming. *If Ava tells Caleb and Tyler I can draw,* she thought, *they'll figure out it was me behind that picture!*

3
REVENGE GETS ROLLING

TYLER and his family were wedged in a booth at The Pancake House. It was Sunday morning after church. Grams was giving Tyler and Caleb belated birthday cards.

"They were on my desk for months. I don't know how I missed them." Grams slid the envelopes across the table.

"No worries," said Tyler. Grams always gave the best birthday cards. They were homemade with a hand-drawn picture and a wad of cash. Tyler treasured them. He kept all eleven in his nightstand. *What did Grams draw for me this year?* Tyler wondered.

Caleb ripped his card open. "This is great," he said. But Caleb's tone sounded off.

Tyler scanned the envelope resting in his hands.

"TYLER" was spelled out in shaky letters. Inside he found a store-bought card with the Easter Bunny and a basket of eggs. Underneath, Grams wrote "HAPPY BIRDAY!" She had also included a hundred dollar bill. The money was nice, but Tyler felt ill. *Grams got Easter and my birthday confused?* he thought. *And she misspelled "birthday?"*

Before Tyler could say anything Ava leaned over and looked at the card. "That's so… sweet."

"Y-yeah, Grams," Tyler stammered. "Thank you so much."

"You're welcome, dears." Grams smiled as the twins hugged her.

Grams used to be a famous pet portrait artist. Before Tyler and Caleb were born, Coffee Pot Corporate used one of her cat pictures to launch their new Perk-Up blend. All of America recognized Grams's famous cat holding a latte.

But now, Tyler looked at that Easter card and wondered. *Did Grams forget she was an artist?* He had to find out. "Maybe later today you could give us another art lesson, Grams," suggested Tyler. "I'd love that."

"Yeah," said Caleb. "I still suck."

"Don't say 'suck,'" Grams said quickly. Then she stared into the depths of her coffee mug. "I don't know where my paintbrushes are," she admitted. "I think the cleaning lady stole them."

"That's horrible!" Tyler exploded. "Dad! You've got to do something. Call the retirement home and tell the manager. Grams, I'm so sorry that happened—"

Mr. Adler coughed. "It's okay, Tyler. I'll be sure to straighten this out later but not right now. The pancakes are coming."

Everyone leaned back in their seats to make room for the waitress who held a giant tray. Ava had ordered a German apple pancake that smelled like heaven. Tyler and Caleb got the Lumberjack Special: a stack of griddle cakes, toast, hash browns, bacon, and sausage.

"That's a lot of pork," their mom said when she saw the twins' plates.

"Mom," Caleb grumbled. "It'll be fine."

Meanwhile, Tyler's mind was stuck on repeat. "Dad," he tried again. "You've got to call Cascade Brooks immediately. How could the staff steal from Grams? It's not fair—ouch!" Tyler jerked. Somebody had kicked him under the table. "Who did that?"

"Oops. Sorry," said Caleb. He looked at Tyler hard, like he was trying to communicate telepathically. All Tyler saw was his own face staring back.

"Mom," Mr. Adler told Grams, "when we take you home today we'll help you look for your art supplies, okay? If we can't find them I'll buy you new things *and* talk to the manager. I'm not going to let anyone steal from you. I promise."

"That would be wonderful, Walter. Thank you. I keep losing things and…" Grams's voice tapered off. Her eyes were watery.

Finally Tyler understood. *Grams can't remember where she puts things anymore and she thinks she's being robbed.* A silence blanketed the table like a pancake.

Grams lived in an assisted living apartment at Cascade Brooks, "the premier retirement home for loved ones with mild memory impairment." But if things got worse Grams would have to move to the Alzheimer's ward, which was like permanent daycare for old people.

"It'll be okay, Grams," Caleb said. "You'll see."

"Yeah—and hey. Do you know who else likes to draw?" Ava asked a bit too brightly. "Brian's little sister Sydney. She's a really great sketch artist."

"What?" Caleb asked.

"Yeah." Ava nodded. "Sydney's even better than you, Tyler."

"No way," Caleb growled. "That's not possible."

"Or is it?" Tyler asked, looking at his brother. He didn't have to be a mind reader to know what Caleb was thinking this time. *Holy cow! It was Sydney!* Tyler slammed down his fork and splattered the syrup.

CALEB and Tyler arrived at school the next morning packing an arsenal of origami stars with "OPEN ME" written on them in big black letters. By recess, the cartoons of Sydney were everywhere. "FREAK SHOW ON WHEELS," Tyler wrote, right next to three versions of Sydney. The fourth grade version looked normal with Sydney riding a bicycle in jeans and a t-shirt. The fifth grade version looked like a ten-year-old vampire on rollerblades: black hoodie, shorn head, and black finger nail polish.

The last picture showed Sydney in black and white striped tights, a purple dress, a black leather jacket, and white blonde hair colored with pink marker. Tyler drew her cruising away on her scooter with a scowl.

"Freak Show" is right, Caleb thought. So why did he feel like a dog? Maybe it was because when the bell rang Sydney walked into Mr. Baker's class with her hands bunched into fists, making eye contact with no one but Emma. Sydney took her seat by the window and put her binder up like a barricade, her head barely visible. Caleb looked over at Tyler and saw his brother smile. When Tyler caught Caleb's eye, he silently signed "c." Caleb made a "t" back, like always. But he started to sweat.

When Mr. Baker's back was turned, Drake leaned over to Sydney and whispered, "Hey, Freak Show. Need any axle grease?"

"Shhhhh!" Emma hushed. Then Mr. Baker whipped around and gave Emma the evil eye.

When Mr. Baker turned back to the whiteboard, Drake bugged Sydney again. "Freak Show," he whispered, "are you there?" Drake rapped on Sydney's binders, and her whole barricade knocked over.

"Miss Taylor?" Mr. Baker faced the class again. "Is there a problem?"

Sydney looked up from the floor where she scrambled to pick up paper. "No, Mr. Baker." Her whole face was clenched. She carefully assembled her binder wall again.

When Drake rocked back in his chair and surveyed the classroom like he was king, Caleb wished Drake's chair would fall over.

Then Sydney slipped a drawing in the plastic window of her walled-up binder. She'd drawn it quickly in big thick Sharpie. It was a cartoon of Drake sitting on a hospital bed with his finger stuck up his nose. The caption read, "HELP DOCTOR! I CAN'T GET IT OUT!"

Caleb laughed so hard he almost barked. Tyler joined in. Emma, the guys from the soccer team—nobody held back.

Mr. Baker slammed down his dry erase marker. "What is going on now?" he shouted.

But Sydney's binder was already down flat. She stared at Mr. Baker like a perfect angel.

Moxie, Caleb thought. *That's what Grams would call it.*

Was Caleb impressed? Yeah, he was impressed. Did that mean he liked her?

EMMA stood in the girl's washroom, trying to calm her best friend down, after Sydney had locked herself in a stall. "Sydney, come on. You're stronger than this. This is nothing." Emma looked under the door and talked to Sydney's feet. "Do you think this is about that laxative cartoon?"

"It's a caricature!" Sydney's voice was muffled. "Why do people mix that up?"

"Come on out so you can explain it to me."

Sydney banged open the door. "Emma, something bad happened." The violet smudges under her eyes from crying matched her purple wicked witch tights.

Emma curled her toes in her boots. "Tell me so I can help."

Sydney twisted a strand of blonde hair around her finger. "Brian has a girlfriend."

"A girlfriend? Oh my gosh, Sydney, you really had me scared. That's no big deal, right? Your brother's had lots of girlfriends."

"You don't get it," Sydney said. "Brian's new girlfriend is Caleb and Tyler's big sister Ava, and she saw one of my drawings!"

"Whoa! Of what?"

Sydney turned on the water and viciously pumped the soap. "Call it 'A Montage of Princess Diarrhea.' The point is she probably told Caleb and Tyler I can draw. Now they've gotten even."

Sydney put on a brave face, but Emma could see the cracks behind it. Emma didn't care what Sydney did with that laxative cartoon. *That was nothing,* Emma thought. *Making fun of how somebody handles her dad dying is a whole different story.*

Emma stepped closer to the mirror so her face was right next to Sydney's. What she was about to suggest was really scary because Emma hated being the center of attention. But she'd do it for Sydney. "Don't worry. I've got an idea. Let's go to Miss Klimey's class and borrow her chair."

"A chair?" Sydney asked. "Why?"

"You'll see," Emma said. "It rolls."

TYLER didn't give a rip if Sydney knew that picture was from him. He wanted her to feel what it was like to have everyone mock you. Now he was sitting next to Caleb in the cafeteria. The whole place smelled like chicken nuggets.

"Did you see how fast Sydney drew that picture of

Drake?" Caleb helped himself to Tyler's snap peas and dumped his carrot sticks on the table. "I thought Drake was going to crush something."

"You're not supposed to admire her," answered Tyler. "Freak Show is the enemy."

"The enemy?" Caleb asked. "Look, that poop picture sucked. But now we're even. Fair and square. The cartoon war is over."

"It is definitely not over!" said Drake. He arrived at the table and slammed down his tray.

"Whoa, look!" exclaimed Caleb.

Tyler turned as a hush overtook the cafeteria. Sydney and Emma stood at the doorway. Sydney sat on a rolling desk chair and held a bright red apple. Emma gripped the back of the chair. Both of them stared Whitman Elementary down. "What do you say, Freak Show?" Emma called out. "Are you ready for some lunch?"

"Definitely," Sydney answered. "Let's roll!" Sydney leaned back in the chair, clearly enjoying the ride as Emma pushed her toward Tiffany and Karen. For such a little thing, Emma was strong. Emma pushed the chair so hard that they picked up air as Sydney rolled to the table. Both of them laughed joyfully.

"Here we go again." Drake snorted. "'FREAK SHOW ON WHEELS.'"

But Sydney and Emma had gleams in their eyes like they enjoyed the attention, even Emma who usually acted so shy. When they came to a stop at their table, Sydney took a big crunchy bite out of her apple. Then Sydney threw that apple straight at Tyler, like she was trying to pelt him in the chest.

Tyler barely caught it in time. The apple hit Tyler's hand hard. He felt its shiny skin in his palm, plus the juicy bit where Sydney took a bite. The blood rushed through Tyler's ears and he couldn't hear a thing. So Tyler did the impetuous thing, the thing that's kind of gross if you think about germs too much. Tyler took a bite right back out of Sydney's apple. Then he spit the chunk on his tray. "Game on, Sydney Taylor." Tyler said it as loud as possible. He wanted everyone to hear.

4
MEMORIES STAB THE HEART

SYDNEY really wanted to hit Tyler with that apple the day before in the cafeteria. Now it was Tuesday afternoon and Sydney had moved on to another plan. At the kitchen table with all of her stuff spread out, she came up with something good. It was a caricature of Caleb and Tyler in big-boy diapers.

Sydney rubbed her hands together for warmth. *Almost done,* she thought to herself, *but I need some words.*

Sometimes food helped Sydney think, so she headed to the fridge. All she found was a jar of pickles. Considering all of the insurance money her mom got after Sydney's dad died, there really should have been something to eat besides condiments. But that would require Sydney's mom to go grocery shopping. Instead, Mrs. Taylor spent all her time running her yoga studio or dating her ski-instructor boyfriend. Sydney hated George. He called her "Little Missy."

At least there was a giant bag of sugar. Mrs. Taylor had bought it on a Costco run a couple of years before, and forgot about it in the garage. Sydney had been snacking on sugar one mug-full at a time.

If Brian got his license next month, then maybe the family would finally have some food in the fridge again on a regular basis. Or maybe they would go grocery shopping this Saturday. Sydney's mom promised to stay home all weekend instead of spending her free time with George.

Mrs. Taylor needed to stay home so she could teach Brian how to drive. Brian turned sixteen next month. But so far, the only time he spent behind the wheel was in drivers ed.

Sydney doled out sugar and spun the spoon around the mug. She pulled her bathrobe tight over two fleece jackets. The house was freezing cold, but sugar spurred her inspiration. *I got it!* Sydney was thrilled. She grabbed her pen and added the tag, "WHERE DID OUR BUTT WIPES GO?"

Sydney was printing copies when she heard the front door open.

"What happened to the heater?" Brian stomped into the kitchen.

"I tried to spin the dial, but it won't work."

Brian headed straight for the thermostat. "58 degrees? No wonder it's freezing in here." Brian messed with the dial too. "Huh, that's strange," he said when nothing happened.

"Can you fix it?"

Brian rubbed his hand over his buzz-cut. Then he looked at Sydney and smiled. "Piece of cake. Probably the pilot light went out." Brian walked past Sydney and rumpled the top of her head. But his own shoulders slumped. The pilot light was something their dad used to handle.

Sydney pulled out a fresh piece of paper. She had never sent a letter to Puget Sound Energy before, but now seemed like a good time to start. Sydney prepared to mail them a really pitiful picture of kittens freezing to death.

C ALEB tried to calm his brother down. It was right at the end of recess, which was horrible timing.

"Butt wipes!" Tyler shrieked when he unfolded Sydney's latest airplane.

Caleb clenched his jaw. "We can't let her know it bothers us." He found a spot at the end of the line. Classes streamed back into the building like long lines of ants.

"I'm not letting it get to me. I don't care about Sydney." Tyler stuffed his hands in his pockets. "But it bugs me that her artwork is better than mine."

"At least you can draw," said Caleb. "You got all of Grams's talent."

"I'm not sure about that. But I wish Grams could still give us art lessons like when we were little," answered Tyler. "Grams doesn't even paint any more. It's like part of her is gone!"

Caleb slumped his shoulders. "I try not to think about it." He sped up his step.

Tyler walked faster too. "Every Saturday at Cascade Brooks I keep hoping. Every time we open the door I pray she'll be better."

"Yeah," Caleb said. "Or that at least it will be one of her good days."

"Sometimes it seems like the good days are gone forever."

"Don't say that." Caleb paused for a moment. Then he hurried up again. "Do you think Grams misses us? Do you think she remembers who we really are?"

Caleb and Tyler glanced at each other. Same brown hair. Same brown eyes. Same tanned nose. They were browned all over.

"Misses us, yeah. Of course she does," Tyler said.

"Does that make it better or worse?"

Tyler didn't answer.

"I wish there was a way to love Grams enough so that all her memory could come back," Caleb said.

"Me too." Tyler slapped Caleb on the back, trying to buck him up. They walked towards Mr. Baker's classroom, a solid wall of togetherness.

Caleb saw Sydney staring at him from her desk by the corner. She wore a ninja shirt and a fluffy purple skirt. Caleb tried not to stare back. That ninja shirt was pretty cool.

"Stop smiling at Freak Show," Tyler whispered loudly at Caleb.

"Don't call her that!" Emma sprang to her feet and everyone in the class stared.

Caleb's face drained white. As far as Caleb was concerned, Emma was a grandma-hater. So he lashed out. "Mind your own business, Airhead."

"Ladies and gentleman? Is there a problem?" Mr. Baker asked, holding his coffee.

"No, sir." Caleb sat down at his desk. Then he looked straight forward at the whiteboard. He didn't look at Sydney, he didn't look at Tyler, and he only saw Drake flick origami stars at Sydney out of the corner of his eye. Caleb knew he shouldn't have called Emma that mean name again. But he was positive he wasn't smiling at Sydney. *Tyler totally misread that,* Caleb thought. *I was picturing ninjas, that's all. I can't help it if nunchucks make me smile.*

But then Caleb did sneak a peek at the enemy. He saw Sydney with her blonde hair hanging over her desk, madly scribbling away. Caleb looked toward Tyler and saw his brother sketching hard too. It was like he was caught in the middle of a lightning storm. Caleb felt the tension all over him like he was going to sizzle.

When the bell rang for lunch Tyler and Sydney both rushed to the restrooms. Two minutes later cell phones buzzed as new pictures got texted to every sixth grader with a phone.

Caleb howled when he saw the picture his brother drew of Sydney riding a recumbent bike. She looked like a dorky dad. But Caleb stopped laughing when he saw Sydney's revenge. It was a picture of Caleb and Tyler dressed up in ball gowns. The tagline read, "PLAYING PRINCESS IS TYLER AND CALEB'S FAVORITE SPORT."

I'm wearing a tiara? Caleb freaked. He was so angry he was ready to bite.

EMMA stood in her beautiful and tidy bedroom. Sydney would be over any minute and Emma was making sure everything was perfect. Her room had an aquamarine and gold theme, with shiny white furniture and satin cushions. Emma dusted everything down each day, and made sure the windows sparkled. More light made it easier for her to read.

Mr. Baker had assigned the sixth graders an essay on L. Frank Baum's book *The Wonderful Wizard of Oz*. Emma was loading up her CD player with the audio book when Sydney knocked on the door. "I'm here," Sydney said, swinging it open.

"Great." Emma reached behind her headboard and pulled out a drawing board for Sydney. Sometimes Sydney got pencil shavings all over and Emma didn't want to put her white carpet at risk. Emma sat on the floor with her textbook on her lap. Sydney turned on the desk lamp and settled in to draw. Then Emma lifted the remote and pressed "play."

If Emma concentrated hard, and tracked with a bookmark, she could follow along fine. Sometimes the words started to wobble, but the bookmark really helped. Besides, Emma had listened to the book five times already. That afternoon was about ensuring that Sydney did her homework. It was Thursday, and that paper was due Monday. Of course, making Sydney listen to the book and actually having her write her essay were two different things.

"Pause it," Sydney said after about twenty minutes. "I thought Dorothy had ruby slippers."

Emma looked up from where she sat on the floor. The pattern on her wallpaper wiggled. "That's from the movie," Emma managed to say. "In the book Dorothy's shoes are silver."

Sydney put her charcoal down. "Are you okay? You're rubbing your forehead. Do you need to take a break?"

"I'm fine," Emma said a little too quickly. Sometimes her dyslexia made Emma see double. "But maybe we could take a moment and talk about our essay instead."

Sydney rolled her eyes. "Why would we want to do that? Too bad I can't draw a picture as a report instead of writing an essay."

Emma stood up to see Sydney's sketch. It was a picture of Dorothy, the Scarecrow, the Tin Woodman, and the Cowardly Lion on the Yellow Brick Road. "This is amazing, Sydney. But you'll write a great essay too, right?"

"I haven't decided yet."

"But progress reports come out in December. What will your mom say when she finds out you've been slacking?"

Sydney slammed down her charcoal and little bits went flying. The poor white carpet never had a chance. "The real question is, will my mom even bother looking at my grades?" Sydney asked.

"Sydney." But Emma didn't know how to finish her sentence. It had been bad between Sydney and her mom ever since the accident. Nothing Emma had said helped. So Emma looked back at Sydney's drawing. "What? No flying monkeys? I thought you'd make one look like your mom's boyfriend or something."

"George *is* kind of stinky." Sydney laughed. "Turn the CD back on and I'll get right on it."

So Emma did. But the thing was, because of that two-minute pause talking to Sydney, Emma had lost her place in the book. She moved her bookmark around, trying to get the words to match up with the sound, but she was lost. Emma looked up at Sydney's head bent down over her work. If Emma asked, she knew Sydney would help.

But Emma didn't say a word.

5
STUPID ADULTS SAY STUPID THINGS

SYDNEY woke up Saturday morning and saw her mom wearing doggie pajamas. *Those are a good omen,* Sydney thought. *They're the sign of a cozy Saturday, like the old days.* But Sydney was wrong.

"Do you want some coffee?" she asked her mom, holding up a bag of Perk-Up blend.

Mrs. Taylor ran her hands through her bleached-blonde hair. "No thanks. I've switched to tea." She headed over to a drawer and pulled out a fancy box of tea from Pike Place Market. "Could you put the kettle on, Sydney?"

"Sure thing." Sydney reached for the tap.

Mrs. Taylor's phone buzzed from the pocket of her robe. She read the text and giggled.

"Who's that?" Sydney asked.

"George." Her mom's voice sounded dreamy.

By the time the kettle whistled, Brian was awake and dressed in cords and flannel.

"Since when did you go grunge?" Mrs. Taylor asked him. She sat cross legged on the barstool, dipping her tea bag up and down.

Brian popped a heel of bread into the toaster. "What's grunge?"

"You know, Pearl Jam, Nirvana, scruffy hair and flannel. George and I went to a concert at Key Arena the other night and saw the Smashing Pumpkins."

"You went to a Halloween party?" Sydney asked.

Mrs. Taylor's eyes narrowed. "Don't be smart with me. Smashing Pumpkins is a band." Mrs. Taylor walked over and tossed her tea bag in the trash. Then her phone buzzed and she texted away, lost in her thumbs.

"Get dressed so we can go for my driving lesson," Brian whispered to Sydney. She nodded to him over her cornflakes. "Wear something normal!" Brian cautioned.

A half hour later the three of them stood in the driveway. Sydney was dressed for comfort in cargo pants, combat boots, her spiked leather belt, and a purple thermal shirt with a spider on it.

Mrs. Taylor looked at Sydney from up above. She wore super high-heeled leather boots and a mini-skirt short enough for a high schooler. "Since when did you go goth, Sydney?"

"What?" Sydney asked. "I'm going for urban-pixie-hipster!"

Brian pushed the button and the garage door opened before Mrs. Taylor could respond. There was a twelve-year-old Honda Odyssey that had seen a lot of good times, and a two-seat Porsche Boxter their mom had bought right after the first insurance check came. Sydney hated that convertible. It was too tiny to survive a crash.

Mrs. Taylor slowly walked up to the minivan. "Let's get this over with," she said.

Brian hung back. Sydney didn't rush either. Their family didn't have the best track record with driving. But Sydney rallied. "You'll do great," she said loudly. "I know it." Then she slid open the van door and climbed inside.

CALEB was right there watching when the near-accident happened. It was half time at soccer and he was getting his hat from the car. All of a sudden he saw a minivan screech to a stop, and a Mini Cooper zoom right through the intersection out of nowhere.

Caleb watched as Mrs. Taylor jumped out of the passenger seat of the minivan, ran to the other side, and flung open the door. "You could have gotten us all killed!" she screamed.

A tall, scrawny guy with a short haircut emerged. That's when Caleb realized the driver was Brian, Ava's new boyfriend. "I'm sorry, Mom. I'm sorry," Brian kept repeating.

But Mrs. Taylor would have none of it. "You're a crazy driver who will ruin our lives! I'm never getting behind the wheel with you again!" She pummeled Brian on his shoulders with the palms of her hands.

The whole thing was messed up. Meanwhile, cars lined up, honking, because they were a big old block in the road. Caleb heard the whistle blow from the soccer field. Half time was over. But he couldn't move a muscle. The van door slid open, and Sydney flew out like an avenging ninja.

Sydney lunged at her mom and pulled her off Brian. "You're not allowed!" Sydney yelled at her mom. "You're not allowed to do that!" Sydney's fists were clenched, but Brian didn't move. His arms were glued to his side and he looked straight at the asphalt.

Mrs. Taylor put her hands down. She wore this crazy sweater you could almost see through. It was way too flimsy for October. Her junky makeup made her look freaky. Mrs. Taylor reached into her purse and pulled out her wallet. "Here." She shoved money at Brian. "Pay somebody to teach you. I'm no good at this." Then she got back in the van and drove away, leaving Sydney and Brian standing there alone in the middle of the street.

Caleb heard a throat clear behind him. It was his dad, bundled up in fleece. Mr. Adler watched the whole scene go down too. "Caleb," he said. "Coach wants you on the field."

Sydney turned around. When she saw Caleb her whole face went white. But Brian? He stood there, staring down at the blacktop.

"Go," Mr. Adler told Caleb. "I've got this." Then his dad walked into the street to join Brian and Sydney. "It's okay, buddy," he said to Brian. "It wasn't your fault."

Caleb heard the whistle blow again, up from the field. He knew he should run fast to get there. Tyler and Drake and the rest of them would wonder where he was. But Caleb walked down into the street too. "Hey, Freak Show," Caleb said to Sydney. "Cool shirt."

EMMA used to love Halloween. She and Sydney would dress up in coordinating outfits and their dads would march them around the neighborhood until their pillowcases dragged with candy. Emma's dad never dressed up, but Mr. Taylor used to wear a captain's hat and a shirt with the word "obvious" on it. That was a million years ago. Emma and Sydney still spent Halloween together, but now that they were sixth graders, they decided to pass out chocolate.

Tonight the Silvers were having open-faced fish sandwiches with a side of boiled potatoes. Emma's great-grandparents were Norwegian so sometimes her mom made weird food. Emma knew Sydney was unfazed by this because Sydney was over at the Silvers' house for dinner once or twice a week.

The four of them sat at the dining room table. The furnace clicked on and there was a soft whoosh. Emma moved her feet to the heating vent on the floor and felt her socks warm up.

Mrs. Silver passed out refills of milk. "So, Sydney," she said. "How'd your essay turn out?"

Sydney pushed around food on her plate. "What essay?"

"The one for *The Wonderful Wizard of Oz*," Emma said. "It's due tomorrow."

Sydney stabbed potatoes. "I haven't started yet."

"I hope you will," Mrs. Silver said, fiddling with her napkin. "When I was about six or so, my parents got divorced. I went through a really hard time at school, not knowing if I wanted to bother or not. I was so upset I was even mad at myself."

If Emma could send her mom brain messages she would. *Be careful what you say.* That morning she tried to make her mom understand the truth about Sydney's situation. Sydney's mom no longer cared about being a parent. But Emma's mom refused to believe it! She still thought of Judy Taylor as a mom-friend who was going through a rough time.

Sydney looked at Mrs. Silver with dark eyes. "I'm not angry. And this is totally different."

Mrs. Silver blundered on anyway. "I know, sweetie. But that doesn't mean you don't have things to be angry about."

"My name's not 'sweetie' and I'm fine." Sydney was like the prickly part of Velcro.

But Mrs. Silver, with her round face and puff of hair, was nothing but softness. "Then be nice to yourself," she said. "Keep your grades up and do your homework."

We're two seconds away from my best friend never coming here again! Emma thought. Her neck was so tight it felt like it might crack. The only sound was the hot breath of the furnace.

"Your father was the smartest person I knew," Emma's dad said to Sydney. Mr. Silver still had his work shirt on, the one that read, "Silver Plumbing." "And for someone with book smarts he didn't make a person feel stupid. That's something I always appreciated about him. I bet your dad would be proud of you no matter what grades you got. But he'd also want you to take care of yourself, and show everyone how capable you are."

It was like a dam broke when Mr. Silver said that. Instead of raging like Emma thought she would, Sydney started crying. She let Mrs. Silver hug her.

"I'll go turn the light on for trick-or-treaters," Mr. Silver said. Then he left the table.

"It'll get better," Mrs. Silver said. "It'll get better, I promise."

"How?" Sydney whispered.

"Because you've got a whole bunch of people who love you," Emma offered.

"Your mom too, Sydney," Mrs. Silver added, "even if she's not showing it right now."

Sydney wiped her eyes. "Can we not talk about this anymore?"

"Yeah," Emma said. "Let's go help my dad with the candy."

But what Emma didn't tell Sydney was that she was really excited about her own essay for the next day. Her mom had bought Emma new software for her computer called Magic Dictation. The way it worked was Emma spoke her essay into the microphone, and words popped up on the screen.

Of course, Magic Dictation wasn't perfect. Emma still had to go over her printed-out essay with her bookmark and color-coded pens. Plus, she had her mom read it, and Miss Klimey too.

"I knew you could do this," Miss Klimey had told Emma the previous Friday after reading Emma's essay. "I knew those amazing thoughts and ideas were in that beautiful brain of yours." She hugged Emma so hard her old lady perfume got into Emma's sweater.

The point was Magic Dictation was awesome. Emma's mom wanted to buy it for Emma's dad too, who also had dyslexia. So Emma had a good feeling about her essay. She couldn't wait for Mr. Baker to see what she could do.

TYLER plastered on his best smile to mask his jitters.

"Last week of the season!" Drake said, as the boys walked in line after recess. "If we win on Saturday, we go to the playoffs!"

"Sounds epic." Caleb grinned. "I can't wait."

"Me neither," Tyler bluffed. He followed the other kids into Mr. Baker's room and tried not to notice Emma, who was wearing a soft pink sweater and looked pretty. Ever since Tyler saw Emma push Sydney through the cafeteria in that desk chair, Tyler noticed Emma everywhere. Emma walking to the special ed room. Emma in gym class with her white knee socks. Emma on the sidewalk wearing an enormous pink coat and laughing at something Sydney had said. When Emma laughed, you could see her perfectly straight teeth.

Tyler licked his braces and felt Emma glare at him as he walked by her desk. *Will Emma ever forgive me for those cartoons about Sydney?* he wondered. *November began with a truce!* Things weren't exactly amicable, but Tyler hadn't posted another picture of Sydney, not after Caleb had told him about the previous Saturday with Sydney's mom and the minivan.

"That's messed up," Tyler said when Caleb had told him.

Still, Tyler knew Brian was a good guy, not like some of those losers his sister had dated. When Brian was over at the Adler house for dinner the other night, he taught Tyler how to do a kickturn on his skateboard.

Tyler thought Brian was cool, and he was sorry Mrs. Taylor was messed up and Mr. Taylor was dead. That meant Tyler was sorry for Sydney too. That was why he hadn't drawn any new cartoons. So far the truce was holding and Tyler had been able to concentrate on soccer.

That didn't mean he wasn't still drawing. Right now, for example, Mr. Baker was launching into a lecture about conscientiousness, and Tyler was drawing noses. His own nose was easy. Tyler saw it all the time on Caleb. Long at the top and round at the bottom with a little bulge that stuck out in the middle.

Emma's nose was more difficult. She had a gentle slope and freckles. Tyler zoned in on Emma's nose for a closer look. That's when he realized Emma was shaking. He stopped concentrating on Emma's nose and brought the whole room back into focus.

Mr. Baker strolled up and down the aisle, wearing a yellow shirt. His stomach was so huge he had to turn sideways to squeeze past the desks near the pencil sharpener. "I can hardly believe the incompetence," Mr. Baker said. "These are the worst essays I've ever seen." He passed out papers, face down, desk by desk. "Some of you barely passed." Mr. Baker was at Caleb's desk now, and he slapped down an essay. "Others of you shouldn't rely on spellcheck." Mr. Baker stood next to Karen and she quaked. "Some of you," Mr. Baker continued, heading over to Tyler, "performed nowhere near your potential."

The essay hit Tyler's desk and covered his binder of noses. He turned the paper over and saw a B+. *Are you kidding me? I guess genius is always doubted.* Tyler's stomach gurgled.

Mr. Baker headed over to Sydney's desk by the window. "Clearly many of you did not bother to read your essay before you turned it in." He slammed Sydney's essay in front of her. Mr. Baker moved on before Sydney stuck out her tongue.

"But the worst disappointment," Mr. Baker said, "is from the individual who cheated. Integrity is essential not only in classwork, but also in life. Smart people know it's better to turn in your own work—no matter how lacking —than to plagiarize the words of others." At this, Mr. Baker returned the last essay.

It fluttered down onto Emma's desk.

Did Emma cheat? Tyler didn't buy that one bit.

Emma's nose dripped. Instead of a soft pink color, it was red. Her whole face scrunched up and her shoulders sloped down over her desk like somebody had wacked her from behind.

"Miss Silver?" Mr. Baker asked. "Would you like to be excused?"

Emma whispered so softly Tyler couldn't hear her response.

"What was that, Miss Silver? Do you have something to say for yourself?"

Emma hopped up, knocking papers off her desk by accident. "I didn't cheat. Every word was my own."

Tyler got that sick feeling again, like he could taste barf. He knew Emma was telling the truth even before Sydney jumped to her feet. Tyler looked over at his brother and saw that Caleb was gripping his desk with white knuckles.

"Emma's not a cheater," Sydney declared.

"Miss Taylor, this doesn't concern you. Miss Silver? Where do you think you're going?"

Emma ran off.

Tyler watched Sydney swoop up backpacks and books. Her arms bulged with the detritus of school.

"Miss Taylor, sit back down." Mr. Baker blustered. But Sydney didn't stop moving. "You will be truant!" Mr. Baker shouted when Sydney got to the doorway.

She turned around and looked right back at him. "Mark me truant or give me an F or whatever. I don't exactly care."

The door slammed shut behind her and Mr. Baker snapped his pencil in two.

6
COURAGE FIGHTS BACK

SYDNEY spent last night drawing the wickedest flying monkey ever. She added a pocket protector, a giant belly, and some thick glasses and ended up with the perfect caricature of Mr. Baker. This morning, she left a bunch of copies in the girls' bathroom and some more in the cafeteria.

Now Sydney was stuck in the principal's office.

Ms. Elder rapped her desk with long pointy fingernails. "I've put a call in to your mother, but she hasn't responded yet."

Sydney shrugged. "Have you texted her?"

Ms. Elder's streaky gray hair flew away from her face. "No. The number on your emergency contact sheet didn't work." Ms. Elder adjusted her horn-rimmed glasses and stared down at a manila file folder. "Your paperwork has apparently not been updated in some time."

"So sue me."

"This isn't a joke, young lady. Those cartoons you displayed around school count as bullying. And now you've defamed Mr. Baker."

Sydney looked down at the chipped blue polish on her thumbs. She tried to formulate a plan for what to say. But her brain wasn't exactly working right. It took a lot of fight to make that picture of Mr. Baker. Now she had nothing left.

"What was a smart girl like you thinking?" Ms. Elder asked. Her question was interrupted by a knock. Before she could respond, the door swung open and Mr. Baker's bulky frame took up the limited office space. Tyler was with him.

"Mary," Mr. Baker said. "Here's another one to question."

Ms. Elder raised her pencil-thin eyebrows. "And this would be…?"

"Tyler Adler," said Mr. Baker.

Sydney looked over at the twin to check for the scar. Tyler's dark hair was brushed back and Sydney could just make it out on his forehead.

"Thank you," Ms. Elder told Mr. Baker. "I'll take it from here."

"Let me know if you need anything, Mary." Mr. Baker clicked the door shut behind him.

Tyler didn't look at Sydney. He slouched back in the chair and stretched out his legs. There was a hole in one pant knee, and Sydney saw skin.

"Well then," Ms. Elder began. "Let's talk about these pictures." She held up prints of Drake with his finger in his nose, the twins in tiaras, and Sydney on her scooter. Sydney snuck a glance at Tyler in spite of herself.

"What about the pictures?" Tyler blurted out. "We've got the right to free expression. It's in the Bill of Rights."

Ms. Elder pushed her glasses further up her nose. "I'm not here to talk about the Constitution. Bullying will not be tolerated."

"Sydney and I had some fun. That's all." Tyler turned to look at Sydney, tapping his toe on the linoleum. "What do you think, Freak Show?"

"No name calling!" Ms. Elder practically screeched. "That's exactly what I'm talking about!"

"It's no big deal," Sydney answered. Tyler's defiance warmed her up. His attitude was a shot in the arm. "Princess Tyler and I were only enjoying ourselves."

"Your definition of 'enjoyment' needs revision, Ms. Taylor." Ms. Elder's eyes narrowed as she held up the picture of Mr. Baker as a flying monkey. "This is harassment of the worst possible type and the consequence is suspension."

Sydney looked at Ms. Elder and then at Tyler. His face was greenish, but he gave her a faint smile of solidarity. It was just enough for Sydney to feel alert and engaged. If she had to, Sydney could have knocked over Ms. Elder's entire desk.

"Tell me," Ms. Elder said in a voice like blackness. "Who is responsible for this one?"

"I am." For a moment, Sydney saw her life flash before her eyes. Co-op preschool with her mom. Learning to ride bicycles with her dad. Playing LEGOs with Brian. That awful week when Emma's family helped plan her dad's funeral. Sydney remembered it all.

"No, I did it," Tyler said.

"What?" Sydney looked at Tyler.

"I'm the one who drew that cartoon," Tyler told Ms. Elder. "Not Sydney."

"That's not true!" Sydney sputtered. "It was me!"

Tyler smirked. "No it wasn't. Look at the fineness of detail!"

"Exactly! You could never draw that well."

"That's not true. I've been practicing."

Ms. Elder's eyes bounced back and forth between them like a volley ball. She cleared her throat a few times, but Sydney and Tyler ignored her.

Sydney bunched up her fists. "I'm the one responsible. I'm the one who posted that picture."

"Not on your life," said Tyler. "That cartoon is all me."

"It's not a cartoon. It's a caricature! Why can't people get that straight?"

"Because art is subjective," said Tyler. "That's what my grandma says. And it doesn't matter what you call it —it's really good. Mr. Baker deserves it after what he did to Emma."

"What?" Ms. Elder asked. "What was that about Mr. Baker and Emma?"

Sydney narrowed her eyes. "He humiliated her."

"He attacked her," Tyler added. "And Emma didn't deserve it. She's the most innocent, brave, truthful girl I've ever met. There's no way she's guilty of plagiarism."

Ms. Elder frowned. "I'm aware there is tension between the Silver family and Mr. Baker. But I don't see how that concerns either of you."

"Emma is my friend," Sydney answered. "I'm on her side."

"I'm on her side too," said Tyler. "That's why I drew that picture of Mr. Baker."

"No. That's why *I* drew it!"

Ms. Elder took off her glasses. "Well. If both of you take credit then both of you will be punished." She clicked her glasses shut in their case. "The consequence is suspension."

Sydney didn't care one bit. She knew she was doing the right thing. It was called grace. It was called sacrifice. It was called doing something nice for someone because gosh darn it, they could use a break. But she didn't understand why Tyler was there too, risking everything.

"Unfortunately, since both of you claim responsibility," Ms. Elder continued. "I won't suspend either of you. It'll be detention instead. Since you both like art so much, you can report to the drama club after school and paint scenes for the school play."

"Drama club?" Tyler asked. "But I've got soccer practice!"

"Too bad," Ms. Elder said with a chilly smile. "Starting Monday, you're painting sets for something you're both very familiar with: *The Wizard of Oz.*"

Sydney shivered.

CALEB was totally proud of Tyler. He couldn't believe Mr. Baker tried to get Sydney and Tyler suspended over that monkey picture. If Caleb could draw, he would have sketched Mr. Baker with toilet paper hanging off his butt. Unfortunately, Caleb's folks didn't see it that way. At dinner Thursday night, they exploded. Caleb hated watching Tyler come under fire.

"You were almost suspended!" Dr. Adler said. She wore pink scrubs because she was an OBGYN and could be called away to deliver a baby at any moment. "What were you thinking?"

Tyler shot back his answer. "I was thinking Ms. Elder is lecturing me about bullying, when the real bully is Mr. Baker."

"So what?" his dad asked. "You didn't draw that cartoon. The smart thing to do would be to stay out of it." Mr. Adler cut a quick glance at Brian, who was joining them for a home-cooked meal. "Sorry, buddy."

Brian shook his head and loaded his fork with teriyaki. "No worries."

Caleb couldn't get over how weird it was to have Sydney's brother right there at the kitchen table. He bet when Ava invited Brian over for dinner, a family blow-out wasn't what she had in mind.

Tyler looked red with anger. "I didn't do this for Sydney. I did this for justice."

"Justice?" Mr. Adler asked. "What does justice have to do with this?"

"Everything!"

"You weren't there, Dad," said Caleb. "You don't know what Mr. Baker is like."

"He's a jerk," Ava added in a superior tone that was pure big sister. "I remember."

"You weren't there either!" Mr. Adler told his daughter.

Ava shrugged. "It doesn't matter. I know Mr. Baker's a bully who doesn't like girls."

"Well that's ridiculous," said Dr. Adler. "If Mr. Baker's

teaching style is so problematic, why is he still a teacher?"

"Beats me," Ava answered. "But if Tyler and Caleb say Mr. Baker was being harsh to Sydney and Emma, then I believe them."

"Yeah, Dad," said Tyler. "Why won't *you* believe I did the right thing?"

Mr. Adler squeezed his eyes shut and then opened them again. "Because," he said, "just because a teacher is a bad teacher, it doesn't mean you can't learn from him."

Tyler threw down his napkin. "Who says I'm not learning?"

"Who says it's okay to watch Mr. Baker treat girls like crap?" Ava added.

"Who says Sydney didn't do the right thing to begin with?" asked Caleb.

Dr. Adler held out her hands like she was trying to calm down a nervous new parent. "Whoa, guys. Let's breathe and work through this." Then she looked at her husband. "One detention doesn't mean Tyler's a juvenile delinquent. And if Ava is right about Mr. Baker being mean to girls, then I have a problem with that. Brian, where's your sister tonight?"

"Sydney's at Emma's for dinner. I wouldn't have come here otherwise." Brian looked at Ava really quick. "I mean, I would have wanted to, but I don't like leaving my sister alone."

Caleb couldn't stand watching Ava share a gooey, romantic moment with Brian. *I wish my sister was ugly,* Caleb thought. *It would make my life as her brother a lot easier because she wouldn't go through so many boyfriends.*

Brian turned his head and looked at Tyler. "Thank you for sticking up for my sister."

"I didn't do it for Sydney," Tyler said stiffly. "I did it for Emma."

"Well, thank you for Emma too. She's like my bonus sister." Brian crumpled his napkin in his hand. "Sydney and I owe the Silvers a lot. So thanks, Tyler, for standing up for Emma. I wasn't there and I didn't see any of it, but I'm positive you did the right thing."

EMMA sat up straight and crossed her ankles. But inside she was thinking, *Please don't let anyone see me cry.* Tears were actually going down her throat instead of out her eyes. That's how hard she was trying to hold it together. Emma was in Ms. Elder's office with a whole bunch of adults. Her mom and dad were there, plus Miss Klimey, Mr. Baker, and Dr. Chang from the special ed office.

Her whole family had gotten up at five a.m. to have everything ready for this meeting. Emma packed her lunch, dressed up, and loaded down her backpack. Mrs.

Silver gathered a huge pile of paperwork and Mr. Silver wore the polo shirt Emma gave him last Christmas that he hated. Emma's mom had a private lawyer on speed dial. Mrs. Silver's cellphone was their secret weapon.

Her dad planned some special tactics too. At the start of the meeting he pulled out his phone and sat it on the conference table. "I'd like to record this conversation so I can review it later." Or in case Mrs. Silver wanted to forward the recording to their lawyer.

Miss Klimey looked at Emma's dad and nodded her head. "Excellent idea, Mr. Silver. This is such a wonderful opportunity to put our heads together and make sure everyone can support Emma." She gave Emma a warm smile.

Dr. Chang cleared his throat and launched in. "Well, then. We're here today to decide if Mr. Baker's class is the best placement for Emma. Mr. Baker has expressed concern over Emma's ability to keep up with the workload."

Emma's mom looked fierce. "And we are concerned about Mr. Baker accusing our daughter of plagiarism and publicly humiliating her."

Mr. Baker grunted. "I've been teaching thirty years and never once have I humiliated a student."

"My daughter left your class in tears." Mrs. Silver narrowed her eyes.

"Proof that regular-ed is too difficult for her," retorted Mr. Baker.

"That shows more about your teaching style than anything else," said Miss Klimey

"My teaching style?" Mr. Baker blustered. "Are you accusing me of something?"

Miss Klimey turned the same color as her purple turtleneck. "Children are not widgets! You can take a student whose brain is different and try to cram her into your widget machine, but it won't work. That doesn't mean she is lazy or has a character deficit. That doesn't mean the girl's not capable. She's just a different type of widget. Maybe she's a gizmo!"

"And gizmos don't belong in my class!" Mr. Baker snapped. "I've taught almost one thousand students and I know Emma is not cut out for my advanced material. She's simply too slow."

"Are you kidding me?" Mr. Silver said, his voice low and terrible. "Did you really call my daughter 'slow?'"

Dr. Chang cleared his throat. "Let's take a moment here and regroup. I feel like we should look at some evidence."

Ms. Elder opened her mouth to speak when Miss Klimey interrupted. "The evidence said Emma wrote an outstanding essay and Harry made the whole class think she cheated."

"She did cheat," said Mr. Baker. "There's no way Emma could have written that essay on her own."

"Actually," Dr. Chang said, fighting to get a word in edgewise, "I have no doubt Emma is capable of writing that essay." He was a small man, with a shiny bald head and rumpled shirt. Dr. Chang was the only calm person in the room.

Mr. Baker's mouth fell open, and Dr. Chang continued.

"Emma's IQ scores from my assessments in September show she is gifted. In fact, she is highly gifted. At the district office, we call students like Emma 'twice exceptional' because she is highly gifted with dyslexia." Dr. Chang's eyes twinkled as he looked at Emma. "You have a very special brain, Emma. It needs careful tending."

I'm smart? For real? As the words sank in Emma had trouble believing them.

Miss Klimey slammed her hand on the table. "I knew it!"

Dr. Chang smiled at her response. "Passion, curiosity, self-motivation, and friendship are what matter in life, not filling in bubbles. But with a little bit of accommodation, Emma can perform well on standardized tests too."

Mrs. Silver grabbed Emma's hand. "Emma wrote her essay by speaking into the computer. That's what helped her get words on paper."

"An excellent idea," said Dr. Chang. "Although you'll have to give me the name of the software programs you used because sometimes those applications don't work very well."

"It's called Magic Dictation," said Emma, finally finding the courage to speak.

"That's cheating," sputtered Mr. Baker.

"No, it's not!" said Miss Klimey. "Emma's allowed to use computers to help her with work. It says so in her file."

Mr. Baker cracked his knuckles. "I don't care what her file or her IQ test says. Ability is different than performance. In all of my multiple assessments of Emma, there is nothing to show that she can keep up."

"Show him," Mrs. Silver said to Emma. "Show him what you can do."

Emma's talent for memorization was her own secret weapon. Or maybe her brain was like a tape recorder, and what went in stayed there like a dam until somebody called upon Emma to spill the information out.

Ms. Elder, Dr. Chang, Miss Klimey, and Mr. Baker all stared at Emma in anticipation. Mrs. Silver squeezed Emma's hand. Emma looked at each one of them.

"It's okay, Emma," said her dad. "Go for it."

And so Emma said the words inside her. "Chapter One of *The Wonderful Wizard of Oz*. 'Dorothy lived in the midst of the great Kansas prairies, with Uncle Henry, who was a farmer, and Aunt Em, who was the farmer's wife.'" The words Emma memorized after all of those times listening to her CD player poured out. "'Their house was small, for the lumber to build it had to be carried by wagon many miles,'" Emma recited. She spoke for five whole minutes until she reached the line, "'The little girl gave a cry of amazement and looked about her, her eyes growing bigger and bigger at the wonderful sights she saw.'"

Dr. Chang clapped and everyone but Mr. Baker joined in.

"I told you," Miss Klimey said, wiping tears off her cheek. "I told you."

Mr. Baker shifted in his chair.

"I think," said Mr. Silver, reaching over to turn off his phone, "this meeting is over."

Emma looked down at the tiny leather bows on the tips of her shoes and released the smallest of smiles. If she had to, she could have kept going.

Emma could have recited the entire book.

7
TEAMWORK SUCKS

TYLER had detention every day after school painting scenery for the school play starting the following week. But right now it was a Sunday afternoon so cold that Tyler's underwear felt frosty. Moms and dads and little sisters were huddled on the sidelines in mountains of fleece. Tyler could hardly see the players because the misty fog was ten parts rain and ninety parts miserable. But the real bummer was that it was Tyler's last game of the season and he had spent fifty-five minutes on the bench.

"One more goal!" Coach yelled as the referee blew a whistle signaling a time out. "One more goal and we're in the city playoffs!" Caleb and Drake came back to the benches for a quick sip of water.

Caleb wiped off his face with a towel. He was covered

with mist and sweat, so it was hard to tell what he was wiping. "You still haven't played?" he asked Tyler. "Man, that's so unfair. You're every bit as good as Drake."

"No, I'm not."

Caleb threw down his towel. "Of course you are. You and me, Tyler. We've come this far together. Double the power. Double the awesome."

"No," Tyler answered. "Not anymore." He stared out into the mist.

The whistle blew again. "Adler," Coach yelled, pointing to Tyler. "Get in the game! You're forward!"

Tyler felt jittery as the adrenaline pumped through him.

But Caleb smiled. "Go get 'em!" Caleb held up his pinkie, signed "t," and winked.

Then, when Tyler started running out towards the field, Coach saw the back of his jersey. *Tyler Adler, Number 9.*

"Tyler Adler?" Coach called out, confused. "I meant Caleb!"

Tyler pretended not to hear. Unfortunately, Coach's lack of confidence rattled Tyler. The grass felt slippery, even with his cleats. The old familiar taste of barf wafted up from Tyler's stomach.

The whistle blew again and the action began.

The game was swift. The ball made circuitous routes all around the field.

"Run, Tyler!" Caleb shouted. "You can do it!"

Tyler felt another surge of adrenaline when he heard his brother, like he'd licked Kool-Aid straight from the packet. It didn't matter how good the other team was. It didn't matter everyone was watching. All that mattered were Tyler's feet and the ball.

Tyler muscled his way into the melee. He took an elbow to the spleen but kept on going. Tyler focused on the ball and pulled out of the crowd, the black and white dribbling between his feet.

"Shoot!" yelled Coach.

"Strike!" Caleb shouted.

But Tyler didn't hear anything except voices blurring in the background.

He saw the net before him. He saw the other team's goalie lifting up his arms and mouthing the word "N-o-o-o-o!"

Tyler slammed the ball into the goal.

That's when his ears started working again. That's when Tyler heard the crowd go wild. Tyler turned around and saw Drake running straight towards him.

"Amazing, Tyler!" Drake blubbered.

Tyler felt like blubbering too. Because it was awesome. For a couple of brief minutes Tyler was euphoric. And he realized, in that very moment, he hadn't had fun playing soccer in a long time—maybe not since third grade when he and Caleb got to go out for pizza after every game.

It was an epiphany. Somehow, Tyler had let himself slog away at two hours of soccer practice every day for months when he knew all along soccer wasn't fun anymore. It was no fun because Tyler wasn't very good at it, no matter how hard he tried. That goal was a lucky kick. *But the thing is,* Tyler thought. *I'm really good at art. But I've been letting my talent slip away because I've been spending so much time at soccer. And why? To keep up with Caleb? He doesn't keep up with me in art, so why have I drilled myself with soccer?*

The final whistle blew and everyone rushed the field. Caleb, Drake, Coach, and Mr. Adler all gave Tyler high fives.

Tyler knew he had to tell Coach the truth. This was his last game of the season.

Maybe it was his last game ever.

SYDNEY spent all weekend thinking about how Tyler had stood up for her in the principal's office the previous Thursday. Now it was Monday afternoon, and Sydney was in the auditorium for her first day of detention, painting scenery for *The Wizard of Oz*. She wasn't sure how she would get home. Staying late after school meant she would miss the school bus. Brian still didn't have his driver's license and it wasn't like she could call her mom to come pick her up. Sydney wasn't a glutton for rejection.

At least she was there with Tyler. Sydney cut a glance at Tyler, slouched in the purple auditorium seat and sketching something in a notepad. She tried to peek at what he was drawing, but she couldn't see squat.

A crash startled Sydney. She turned and watched the double doors of the auditorium open as Mr. Day, a first grade teacher who was also the drama club coach, made a grand entrance. He wore skinny black jeans, a French-cuffed shirt, and a voluminous scarf wrapped around his neck.

Mr. Day walked down the aisle. "My own design team! I'm thrilled!" He reached the stage and swung his whole body upward in a cat-like motion, so he sat on the edge and faced Sydney and Tyler. "I'm a big fan of your work."

Sydney didn't like being mocked. But was Mr. Day mocking her? It was hard to tell. Sydney wasn't used to teachers who were young, or who could sit crisscross-applesauce.

Mr. Day opened up a leather messenger bag that looked careworn with time. He pulled out Sydney's caricature of Mr. Baker as a flying monkey. "This is a fantastic starting point. I love the realism. I love the authenticity. I love how you made a book that's over one hundred years old relatable to Whitman Elementary."

"Um, thanks," Sydney offered.

Then Mr. Day held up Tyler's original Freak Show on Wheels picture. "And you, Tyler. Satire with words and pictures. It's brilliant."

Sydney grabbed her knees tight. Maybe she didn't like Mr. Day after all.

"—But also cruel." Mr. Day put down the drawings and looked at both of them. "I believe art can make an impact without being hurtful. I mean yes, true art should squeeze our hearts and hurt just a little bit, but in a good way. Do you know what I mean?"

Okay, so Sydney did like Mr. Day. And she thought she knew what he was talking about, but she wasn't exactly sure. Until recently, her art had always been her own. That picture of Caleb and the laxatives was the first time she'd ever experimented with art as a weapon.

Mr. Day leaned in closer. "So, I'm dying to know. What are your plans for the set?"

Tyler turned green. "Our plans? Aren't you going to tell us what to do?"

Mr. Day laughed. "No way. If I told you, I'd be getting in the way of artistic expression. I've got a team of parents building the backdrops for you to paint. So what do you think? What ideas are percolating in there?"

Sydney had a concept, but she was worried it might be stupid.

Tyler swayed a bit and clutched his stomach. "When's all of this have to be done by?"

"Opening Night is February 15th." Mr. Day buckled up his messenger bag.

"Seattle!" Tyler blurted out. "The Emerald City could be Seattle. You know, because that's Seattle's real-life nickname."

Mr. Day's face lit up. "Fabulous!"

Sydney couldn't believe she missed her chance—and that Tyler's idea was so cool. No way would she allow Tyler to have the last word. "Munchkin Land could be Whitman Elementary," Sydney suggested. "The Yellow Brick Road could start at the flagpole out front."

Mr. Day leaped to his feet. "Yes! That would be so modern."

"The witch's castle could be on Mt. Rainier!" Tyler added, his face flushed with excitement.

Mr. Day handed them each a card. "Wonderful. Here's my number. Text me some drawings when you're ready. This is a collaborative process."

Sydney met the moment with skepticism. "I thought this was detention," she said. "I thought we were being punished."

"Principal Elder can call it whatever she wants," Mr. Day said, turning to look at Sydney before he walked away up the aisles. "But I'm calling it a second chance."

I'm not sure I believe in second chances, Sydney thought. Mr. Day took a seat at the back of the auditorium and pulled out papers to grade.

"So, Mt. Rainier?" asked Tyler. "That could be fun to paint."

"Yeah," Sydney lied. "Easy-peasy."

CALEB threw his gear in the back of the SUV and climbed in. Tyler's detention got out ten minutes before soccer practice ended, so Tyler was already in the backseat. As soon as Caleb buckled up he undid his shin guards. Pulling off the Velcro felt good.

"How was practice?" Mr. Adler asked, remarkably cheery for somebody who had chauffeured kids for the past two hours.

Caleb cinched his seatbelt. "I'm not gonna lie. It wasn't the same without Tyler." He held up his sign language "t" and Tyler made a "c" next to him. "How was detention?"

"Just barely tolerable."

Caleb turned his head to look out the window. The second week of November meant five o'clock was dark as dog poop.

But when they drove past a strip mall, Caleb saw a familiar figure walking on the sidewalk, illuminated by light from the grocery store. "Dad! Stop the car! It's Sydney!"

"What?"

"I said, 'Stop the car!'"

Mr. Adler pulled over to the curb immediately. Caleb opened the door before the Honda was parked.

Sydney watched that car door open, inches away. Then she dropped her backpack and ran.

"Freak Show, wait!" Caleb yelled. "We're not kidnappers!" He picked up her backpack.

About ten yards away, Sydney turned around. "What do you want?"

"Nothing," Caleb called. "Need a ride home?"

Sydney stuffed her hands in her pockets. "No. I'm fine." She walked up the sidewalk to collect her stuff.

"But it's late," Caleb said. "And dark."

Sydney practically ripped her backpack from Caleb's hands. "Thanks, but no thanks."

Right then Tyler leaned over and stuck his head out the door. "Get in the car, Sydney." Then he darted back inside.

"Please?" Caleb begged.

Sydney looked at Caleb, and then at Tyler in the backseat, and climbed inside. Caleb went in after her, and Sydney got squished in the middle.

Mr. Adler turned around to say hello. "Brian's little sister! Nice to meet you."

"Nice to meet you too." Sydney put her backpack at her feet and buckled up.

"Where to?" Mr. Adler asked.

"Northwest 99th Street, across from Soundview Park."

"That's only a few blocks from us," said Caleb.

"Yeah." Sydney reached into her pocket and pulled out a buzzing cellphone. "My brother keeps texting me. He wants to know where I am." She quickly typed something back.

"Couldn't your mom pick you up?" Mr. Adler asked.

"Um... not really."

"She must work a lot," Caleb offered.

"Um... yeah."

Caleb saw Sydney twist her spiked metal bracelet around and around her wrist. He wondered if Sydney was telling the truth.

"We sure like your brother," said Mr. Adler.

Sydney stopped spinning her bracelet. "He's the best." Her cellphone buzzed again and she looked down at it and smiled. "Brian's always watching out for me."

"That's the sign of a good brother," Mr. Adler said.

"Yeah," Tyler agreed.

But Caleb didn't say anything. He knew it was crazy, but when Sydney talked about Brian, he felt jealous.

When the SUV pulled up the driveway of the Taylor house, Brian walked down from the porch.

"Thanks for giving my sister a lift," Brian said to Mr. Adler as Sydney climbed out over Caleb.

"I'd be happy to carpool with your mom until this detention situation is over."

"Thank you, Mr. Adler, but I've got it covered," Brian said.

"It wouldn't be a problem," Caleb blurted. "It doesn't have to be a carpool. We could just drive her."

Brian gave Caleb a sharp look. "Good to know," he said. "But no need." He slammed the door shut and rapped on the window. "Thanks again!"

Caleb waved back.

"I hope Ava's nice to that guy," Tyler said as they pulled out of the driveway.

"But not too nice," Caleb added.

EMMA almost didn't get to return to school the next day. Her mom had suggested homeschooling, but Emma wanted to be with her friends. Mr. Silver smoothed things over with his wife to make sure that could happen. But there was one condition: Emma had a brand new iPad with a fully charged battery. The rule was every day she attended Mr. Baker's class, she had to press "Record." That was the only way her mom would agree to let Emma go back to Mr. Baker's room.

"This way you can review lectures at home," her mom had said, "and Mr. Baker will know that if he yells at you again, I'll find out."

Emma had wanted a tablet for ages, but not like this. Dr. Chang had written a note explaining to Mr. Baker why Emma should be allowed to have the iPad on her desk. Mr. Baker wrinkled his nose when he read the letter, like he smelled stinky cheese.

The iPad was on Emma's desk now and Tyler was staring at her. He had a dopey look on his face that made Emma's cheeks burn.

Mr. Baker wrote a bunch of stuff on the board about Mark Twain and Emma laboriously copied it down, even though Miss Klimey and Dr. Chang said it was perfectly acceptable for Emma to take a picture with her iPad.

"Focus on listening," Miss Klimey had said. "Take a picture of the board. Use a keypad when necessary instead of writing things out by hand."

"Exactly," Dr. Chang agreed. "When you type your right hand accesses the left side of your brain and your left hand accesses the right. Use a keyboard whenever possible. All of this focus on handwriting is ridiculous."

But perfect penmanship was one of the few things Emma was proud of. She could write slow, beautifully formed letters in gorgeous script. It took her forever, and she couldn't spell anything right—but her handwriting was beautiful.

"Dyslexia means Emma's brain works differently." That's what Dr. Chang told Emma and her parents. "Emma's brain has learned to compensate for her disability. She has strengths ordinary people can only dream about."

But that was the thing. Emma wished with all her heart she could be ordinary.

That night, when Emma got home from school, she'd really learn. Emma would load the audio-book version of *The Adventures of Tom Sawyer* into her CD player. Then she'd listen and memorize.

But right now she was in the middle of class and swimming. Or maybe it would be better to say Emma was drowning. She splashed in words. Fighting with lexicon and kicking at every letter and syllable on the whiteboard until it pulled her to the bottom and turned her lips blue.

Emma fought hard with her pencil. She copied down notes until her eyes popped out.

Mr. Baker launched into an explanation about Aunt Polly's white picket fence when a loud screech interrupted his lecture. Everyone looked at Emma and her iPad.

Eeek! Emma thought. *Is that the alarm?* Emma had been messing with the clock function last night. She tried to set a reminder to take her vitamins. Emma grabbed her iPad and wiped her finger across the screen.

Only the faster Emma moved her fingers, the more apps pulled up. Emma got confused and accidentally pulled up music. Instead of turning off the alarm, a pop song blasted out.

Emma couldn't breathe. It felt like her own breath strangled her right there in the middle of class with everyone watching. She frantically moved her finger, but nothing helped. If anything, the music got louder.

Emma saw Sydney out of the corner of her eye. Emma heard Tyler's chair scrape behind her. But it was Caleb, one desk over, who reached out to help.

With one flick of his finger, the noise turned off.

Caleb cleared the screen and pulled back the voice recorder. "These things can be confusing," he offered charitably. "I like Kindles better."

"Shall we get back to the lesson?" Mr. Baker asked. "I hate interruptions."

Tyler whispered from behind. "That guy's a butthead."

If Emma's face wasn't already red she would have blushed harder. She gripped her pencil so tight the yellow rubbed off. Then she looked right at Caleb. His University of Washington Huskies sweatshirt looked snuggly. The color purple was calming. Emma gave Caleb her kindest, most grateful smile ever. The type of smile you give somebody who just made your whole world better. *I knew Sydney was wrong about this guy*, she thought. *Caleb Adler is awesome.*

Caleb smiled back. Then he looked across the room at Sydney.

8
NERVES ACT UP

CALEB stood by the auditorium door staring at the sign-up sheet during the tail end of recess. He couldn't believe he was thinking of it, but he decided he might audition for the school play. That weekend was the final playoff game. After that, soccer would be all done until spring. Caleb wasn't trying out for basketball that year because Tyler didn't want to. So drama club it was. *Double the power, double the awesome.*

Caleb would volunteer to help with the sets, but everyone knew Caleb sucked at art. He could be on the stage crew, but that seemed boring. No, if Caleb was going to do this he was going all the way. That meant auditioning for the good boy parts: the Scarecrow or the Tin Woodsman. Anyone but the Cowardly Lion, really. *No way do I want to be the wussy cat,* he thought. Caleb was staring at the audition list when Emma walked up.

"Caleb or Tyler?" she asked.

"Caleb."

"Oh," Emma said. "That makes sense. Tyler wouldn't have time to be in the play since he's spending so much time with Sydney doing the set."

"Yeah," Caleb grunted. Emma's white sweater was so poufy it made her look like a marshmallow.

"Are you going to audition?" Emma asked.

That had been the plan, but now that Caleb was standing in front of the board with Emma, he was reconsidering. "I dunno," he said. "Maybe."

Emma pulled out a pen from her backpack. "I've been thinking about it too." Then she looked at him sideways. "You probably think I'm being stupid."

"Nah." Caleb held tight to his pencil and watched Emma sign up her name under Dorothy. "You realize you're going to have to kiss three dudes at the end, right?"

Emma shrugged. "Quick pecks on the cheek to Dorothy's friends before she clicks her heels and goes home. No big deal." She pocketed her pen in her backpack but didn't walk away. Instead, Emma looked up at Caleb with blue eyes. "How's your grandma doing?"

Caleb didn't know what he was expecting Emma to ask, but it wasn't that. As far as he was concerned, Emma was the girl who laughed at Grams in the Olive Garden and then never apologized for it. "Fine," he said stiffly. Then he quickly signed his name on the board and walked away.

Emma followed him down the hall. "Does she have Alzheimer's disease? Is that it?"

Caleb walked faster. "Yeah." The recess bell sounded. Any minute now long lines of kids would start pouring in from the playground. Caleb decided to go straight to class instead.

"Caleb?" Emma asked, still on his heels. "I know I already apologized about the Olive Garden, but I've got to say it again. I'm so sorry!"

"What?" Caleb stopped dead in his tracks. "What do you mean you already apologized? You did not!"

Emma's lip quivered. "But I did. Don't you remember?"

Caleb shook his head. Was Emma having another airhead moment or what?

"I did say sorry," Emma said. "The day after you… the day after I forgot my lunch code and dropped my tray."

"I don't remember that at all. That's crazy."

"But you said you were sorry too," Emma protested.

Tyler, Caleb thought. *It must have been Tyler pretending to be me.*

"You apologized for calling me 'Airhead.'"

The word stung as if somebody had hit Caleb on the

nose like he was a bad dog. "I don't know what you're talking about. I don't remember you apologizing. But yeah, I am sorry about calling you a name. I shouldn't have done that."

"Oh," said Emma. "Whatever." She turned and walked away. Mr. Baker's class had just entered the hallway and Sydney let Emma cut in line.

Caleb spied Tyler at the end. "Hey, wait!"

"Yeah?"

Caleb fake-punched Tyler in the shoulder. "I need to talk to you," he whispered hoarsely.

Tyler shrugged away. "What's up?"

"Did you pretend to be me with Emma Silver? Did you tell her I was sorry for calling her 'Airhead?'"

Tyler's mouth opened up into a silent 'o.'

Caleb felt like snarling. "Why'd you do it? Why didn't you tell me?"

Tyler threw the question right back at his brother. "Why didn't you tell *me* what happened with Grams at the Olive Garden? I mean, what did happen? I'm still not sure."

"I don't want to talk about it," Caleb growled. They were at the entrance to their classroom. The rest of the kids had already gone inside. But neither brother moved.

Tyler glared. "It couldn't be so bad. Emma's a super nice person. And it was really low of you to call her that awful name."

"No way," Caleb answered. "What's low is pretending to be me and then not telling me about it. We have rules about switching places. The other person is supposed to know."

"Oh yeah? Well then why did you switch places with me at soccer practice? I didn't ask you to do that, and you didn't ask permission."

"Soccer practice! I did that for you! So Coach would let you start."

"But I'm not good!" Tyler protested. "And maybe I didn't want to start."

"You could be good if you tried harder. You just need to stop being a wimp and get your head in the game."

"I'm not a wimp." Tyler's face looked dark and brewing. "And I don't need your help. Let me live my life and I'll let you live yours."

"Fine!"

Both twins were still in the hall. "Gentlemen?" Mr. Baker shouted from inside the classroom. "What's the fuss?"

"And another thing," Caleb whispered harshly. "Don't pretend to be me again, especially not with girls." He turned his back on Tyler and walked inside.

TYLER was still on edge from his argument with Caleb. He hoped art detention would offer some asylum. Tyler spread out ten pictures of Mt. Rainier on the auditorium stage. *I'm not going to be nervous, I'm not going to throw up, and I'm not going to let Mr. Day think Sydney is a better artist than me*, he thought. Tyler had the whole Winkie scene mapped out in his head. Mt. Rainier would be to the left and to the right would be the witch's castle. Tyler was concentrating so hard on his vision, he didn't hear Sydney come up behind him.

"Is this some kind of joke?" she asked. For once Sydney looked almost normal. She wore jeans, black boots, and a long-sleeved red t-shirt. But her blonde hair was tipped with magenta marker.

"What do you mean? Artists use visuals for inspiration all the time. I wanted to make sure we got Mt. Rainier just right."

Sydney balled up her fists. "I know how to draw Mt. Rainier."

Tyler scooted over on the stage so Sydney could see the pictures better. "That's Paradise." Tyler pointed to a meadow with flowers. "A place called Sunrise is on the other side."

"I know." Sydney squatted down to look at the pictures. When she saw one of the visitor's center parking lot, her expression got tight. She held up a picture of parked cars and shoved it in Tyler's face. "A blue Prius? You *are* messing with me!" Sydney threw the picture down and scrambled off the stage.

"What are you talking about, Freak Show? It's just a car."

"A car?" Sydney rocked back and forth in her boots. "You're one sick person, Tyler!" She lunged forward like she might hop up on the stage again. "Who told you? Was it your sister? Did Brian tell Ava about it?"

"What do you mean?"

"Did you look it up on the Internet?"

"Huh?"

"Never mind. I don't exactly care." Sydney spun around and marched up the aisle. Right before she left, Sydney looked back over her shoulder. "You're a real jerk, Tyler Adler! I can't believe I ever thought you were nice."

"What was that about?" Mr. Day was standing backstage by the door to the band room.

Tyler wasn't sure how much Mr. Day had heard. "I don't know. Sydney got mad about some picture." Tyler reached down and held up the photograph of the Mt. Rainier parking lot. "She went on and on about a Prius."

Mr. Day crossed the stage and took a look. "Oh, I see."

"You see what? I don't get it."

Mr. Day handed the picture back, pulled out his

phone, and started typing. "Principal Elder filled me in on Sydney's history. I thought you already knew."

"Huh?"

Mr. Day handed over his phone to Tyler. "Maybe this will explain."

Tyler looked at the tiny screen and swallowed hard when he saw the headline.

Fatal Crash After Mount Rainer Ascent

Robert Taylor, Microsoft engineer and father of two, was killed in a car crash yesterday while driving home to Seattle after his third successful ascent of Mt. Rainier. Taylor, a life-long mountaineering enthusiast, was killed on impact when his Toyota Prius was hit by a Chevy Suburban. Authorities say the Suburban was driven by a man under the influence of alcohol.

Underneath the article was a picture of Mr. Taylor's smashed up car. The hybrid was so mangled Tyler couldn't even tell it was a Prius. But Tyler could still see the blue paint job. Tyler swallowed hard again. All of a sudden he felt thirsty.

Mr. Day sat down on the stage next to Tyler. "Are you okay?" he asked.

Tyler tried to remember the last time he'd drunk water. He felt parched, like he hadn't been hydrated for days. Tyler handed the phone back to Mr. Day and zipped open his backpack. He tore through it to find his water bottle. When he did, Tyler gulped down water so hard he almost choked. He drained the bottle fast, and the last few drops dribbled down his chin. Panting, Tyler put the cap back on and shoved it in his bag.

"Feel better now?" Mr. Day asked.

Tyler bunched up the Mount Rainer pictures and stuffed them in his bag. "I'm fine." He zipped the zipper so hard he almost caught his thumb. "I've got to go to the bathroom, that's all."

"Okay," said Mr. Day. "After that, come back and get to work. I'll go find Sydney."

When Mr. Day said that, Tyler felt like a jerk. *I'm the one who should go find Sydney*, he thought. *Not Mr. Day.* But all Tyler could handle was rushing to the bathroom. All he could deal with was his exploding bladder.

And he was thirsty. Tyler was so thirsty it hurt to talk.

SYDNEY didn't need Tyler to show her pictures of Mt. Rainier to remember. She could draw Paradise or Sunrise, or Olympic National Park, or the Cascades—Sydney could draw every mountain in Washington State if she had to. When she was little, Sydney's dad used to take her and Brian up into the woods. Sometimes Sydney's mom would come too, but she wasn't a big fan of dirt. Usually it was just Mr. Taylor and the kids. Brian would tromp along the path swiping down nettles with a switch, and Sydney would ride in her dad's backpack. That's how little she was.

That's how old the memory was.

In fact, hiking with her dad was Sydney's earliest memory. If she closed her eyes she could still see things with her fuzzy three-year-old brain. She could still look across her dad's balding head at the ferns along the path, or rest her head on her dad's shoulders and fall asleep in the backpack.

But that was a long time ago. Now she was sitting on cold concrete, leaning against the outside wall of school, and waiting. Sydney texted Brian that detention got out early (which was sort of true). She knew her brother would come. *Please don't let me cry*, Sydney thought. But she couldn't help it. The tears rolled down her cheeks.

"Mind if I sit down?"

Sydney saw two shiny loafers standing next to her. She looked up and saw Mr. Day in a wool pea coat. Sydney wiped her nose across her sleeve. "Whatever." But she scooted over and made room for him under the awning.

Mr. Day sat down on the ground, reached into his pocket and offered Sydney his handkerchief. "Do you want to talk about it?"

Sydney blew her nose hard. "No." She unfolded the

handkerchief and looked at the corner not covered by snot. There was an elaborate cursive "D" embroidered in green. "You have monogrammed handkerchiefs?"

"Yeah," Mr. Day said. He waved her off when she offered it back. "Keep it. You might need it later."

"Where do you buy handkerchiefs? And how do you get your name on them?"

Mr. Day smiled. "There's a whole world out there, Sydney. Handkerchiefs, fashion, theater, art… There are so many wonderful things out there in life waiting for you to find them. A talented, creative person like you is going to find them all."

Sydney picked at her blue nail polish. "Most people think I'm a freak show."

"Sometimes that's a good thing. It means you're special."

"I don't feel special. I just feel angry."

Mr. Day loosened his scarf. "It's okay to feel angry. You'll probably be angry about what happened to your dad for the rest of your life. But you also have to look for the things and people that make you happy to be alive. That's what you need to focus on, Sydney. Not your rage."

"What if rage is all I've got?"

Mr. Day waited a moment before answering. "You always have a choice. The world is full of light and darkness. There's a Chinese proverb that says, 'Light a candle instead of curse the darkness.' It means you can choose to make things better instead of dwelling on the negative. But first you have to figure out what type of person you want to be."

Right then Brian rolled up on a bicycle. It was a two-seater, with red and white flashing lights.

"It looks like your ride is here." Mr. Day said.

"What about detention?"

Mr. Day smiled. "Take the day off. But tomorrow, I expect good things from you. Prepare to be brilliant."

EMMA would rather be grilled than stand up on stage and have everyone stare at her, but she couldn't ignore Miss Klimey's reasoning. "Audition for the school play," Miss Klimey had told Emma. "You're a smart girl who's going to go to college someday. Performing in *The Wizard of Oz* would look really good on your record. You've already got the whole book memorized. Learning lines should be a snap."

Now it was Friday afternoon at lunch. Only instead of being in the cafeteria with her friends, Emma faced a sea of critics. Mr. Day, parent volunteers, and the drama club were skewering Emma with their judgment. It was her turn on stage.

"Emma Silver." Mr. Day read from his clipboard. "Your solo please."

Emma shuffled forward in pink ballet flats. She tugged her sweater down over her jeans and stood up straight. Emma wasn't really a singer, but she had practiced her song a hundred times in front of her bathroom mirror. A few moments later when Emma launched into "Somewhere Over the Rainbow" her voice was clear and sweet. Emma continued all the way until the end. She offered every inflection and emphasis from the CD she'd memorized. Mimicry wasn't the same thing as acting, but it was close. She tried to remember what Miss Klimey had told her and made eye contact with the audience. Emma's voice hitched a bit when she saw Caleb, but she kept going anyway.

Mr. Day clapped with enthusiasm. "Excellent, Emma. You may take a seat."

Emma felt her cheeks flush. She tried not to slip as she stepped down from the stage. When her feet hit solid floor, she felt a surge of confidence. *I'll be brave,* she thought. *I'll sit next to Caleb Adler.* Emma walked over to the empty seat next to Caleb and sat down, placing her backpack neatly over her toes.

"What's a solo?" Caleb whispered.

"What?"

"A solo. What is it?"

Emma was shocked, not so much by the question, but

that Caleb needed her help. "It's when you sing a song all by yourself," she whispered. Emma watched as Caleb's face fell.

"But I don't have a song prepared. I thought we'd read lines from the script."

"Oh."

Caleb reached down and grabbed his backpack. "This was a stupid idea. I'm gonna go."

Emma placed a hand on his sweatshirt. "Wait! You've got to be able to sing something."

"But I don't know any songs!" Caleb leapt to his feet.

Mr. Day glared at them both with his finger at his lips.

"Weren't you and Tyler in Cub Scouts?" Emma whispered.

Caleb paused, and then slowly sank down into his chair. "Yeah. There is this one song I remember."

Emma gave Caleb a smile.

When Mr. Day called for the next volunteer Caleb raised his hand and bounded up the steps to the stage. Emma watched as Caleb ripped the microphone right off the stand. "I'll be singing my favorite song from Fire Mountain Camp," he announced. "It's called 'Great Big Globs of Greasy, Grimy, Gopher Guts.'" Caleb looked up into the horizon and reached out his hand.

What came next was the most disgusting song Emma had ever heard. But when Caleb finished, he jumped off the stage to boisterous applause. Caleb ran back to his seat and slammed down, right next to Emma.

Emma felt wiggly, like an electric current had jolted right through her.

Caleb leaned his head next to her, so close his shaggy brown hair brushed her cheek. "Thanks. I owe you one."

"No big deal," Emma answered. But she blushed hard.

9
BETRAYAL BITES

CALEB dripped with sweat and felt every muscle ache. He had a cut across his eyebrow that stung. Two of his teammates were down for the count with sprained ankles. This game was going nowhere fast. The score was five to four with four minutes left on the clock, and they were losing. "Over here!" Drake yelled.

Caleb passed the ball and watched in frustration as the other team intercepted. The soccer field was wet and miserable.

"Tear 'em up!" Tyler yelled from the sidelines. He was warming the bench in solidarity. Tyler was no longer allowed to play because detention made him miss practice. "Get that ball back!"

Caleb ignored his brother. Normally Tyler's support

gave Caleb energy. But not today. Today it ticked him off. These past few days with Tyler had been awful. Ever since their Wednesday showdown, Caleb circled Tyler like he was the enemy. Every time Caleb looked at his brother, he wanted to snarl. Caleb hadn't even told Tyler his big news. Yesterday he got a callback for *The Wizard of Oz*. He'd find out on Monday if he got a part.

But right now, Caleb had more important things to focus on. This was the final playoff game. If they lost this match, they were done. The grass was so muddy that every dash, every run, was another opportunity to slip. It took dogged determination to keep going, but Caleb kept running hard.

"Over to you!" Drake kicked a wild shot that flew over the field. Before it could fall out of bounds, Caleb headed it back in. Then he leapt forward, took control of the ball and moved up field towards the goal.

Drake's dad screamed furiously. "Shoot!" he yelled. "We can still tie this thing if you score!"

Caleb ran further and further up the undefended field. The goal was wide open in front of him. The goalie braced for impact. This was Caleb's chance. If Caleb could make this goal, the team would go the regionals.

Caleb pulled his leg back. He told himself: *Don't blow it!* Then he swung his right foot forward making strong contact with the ball.

Only something went wrong.

His right foot hit the ball, but his left foot slipped in the mud. The ball shot off askew, ricocheting off the metal frame of the goal. Caleb slammed down into the ground. At first he thought he was dead. Then the next moment, Caleb wondered if his lungs were crushed. Then he was gasping too hard to think about anything at all. Caleb writhed in the mud and the cold wetness didn't even hurt. He suffocated.

After an eternity of dying, Caleb felt a brisk hand rub circles on his back.

"It'll be okay, Son. You got the wind knocked out of you is all."

A sharp spike of air shot through his chest as Caleb's lungs reopened. He opened his eyes again and saw his mom's face, and then Tyler's, crouched over him. Coach was there too, and he was the one talking.

"Take a moment to shake it off," Coach said, "and then get back in the game. We've still got three minutes to win this thing."

Dr. Adler's eyes flashed fire. "Absolutely not! He might have a concussion. Play somebody else."

"But—" Coach began.

"No buts!"

Caleb's eyes came into full focus now. His power of breath returned. "I can do it," he rasped out.

"See?" Coach said. "We can still win. Drake and Caleb can do this!"

"Drake?" Dr. Adler asked. "This has nothing to do with your kid. This is about mine. I'm the mom, I'm a doctor and I say he's not going to play. I'm taking Caleb home to make sure he doesn't have a concussion."

"A concussion? That's ridiculous! All he did was slip. Three minutes left and we'll be city champs."

"Win it with somebody else!" Dr. Adler cradled Caleb's arm and lifted him carefully to his feet. "Not too fast," she said softly. "Slow and steady."

Now that he was upright, the whole field spun. Caleb's head rolled a bit and Tyler clamped onto his other arm. "Don't worry," Tyler said. "I got you."

Caleb was too out of it to shake his brother off. If it weren't for Tyler and his mom, he probably would have fallen over.

"Number 9!" Coach said to Tyler. "You're in this thing after all."

"What?" Tyler jerked. "Not me!"

Caleb grimaced. His words came out hoarse. "Stop being a butthead, Tyler. Just go out there."

"You can do it," their mom said. "We'll be in the car waiting."

Caleb staggered a bit when Tyler let go of his arm, but he felt better. Good enough now he didn't want his mommy holding his arm, especially in front his friends.

"Don't suck," Caleb said as Tyler walked away with the team. Then Caleb lurched forward and fell.

"Caleb!" his mom cried. She knelt over him and brushed hair out of Caleb's eyes. "Just rest a bit, honey, before we walk to the car. Otherwise I'm calling an ambulance."

"Un, uh." Caleb mumbled. "No ambulance. Just give me a sec." From his grassy vantage point he watched the last minute of the game. Drake shot Tyler an easy pass and his brother missed it by a mile, blowing the chance to score a tie-breaking goal.

The whistle blew sharply. *What the heck? Tyler just lost us the game!*

EMMA was ridiculously excited. She actually felt bubbles on the inside of her heart. Emma double checked the cast list posted on the auditorium wall one more time. She zoned in on her name: "Emma Silver – Dorothy Gale."

"So?" Sydney asked. She stood there waiting. "Did you get something?"

Emma turned around, flushed pink with pleasure. "The lead," she said. "I'm Dorothy!"

"Sweet!" Sydney held up her hand for a high five and the girls smacked palms.

"I can't believe it," Emma said. "I can't believe Mr. Day picked me!"

Sydney rolled her eyes. "I can't believe you'd say that. Of course he'd pick you."

The girls turned to walk back from recess. As they did, one of the twins approached the board. Emma still couldn't tell Caleb and Tyler apart.

"What's Caleb doing reading the cast list?" Sydney asked.

"He auditioned with me," Emma answered.

"That doofus? Did he get a part?"

Emma wrinkled her eyebrows. "I don't know. I didn't remember to check." Emma paused, mid-step, and turned around. She looked back and saw Caleb read the board.

"The wussy cat?" he shouted. "I wanted to be the Scarecrow!"

Emma's face drained of color until she was grayish.

"Son of a biscuit," Sydney blurted out. "You're going to have to kiss Caleb!"

Emma wished Sydney had been a lot quieter, because Caleb turned and looked right at them.

"On the cheek, right?" he called. "No big deal."

"Yeah. No big deal." Emma turned on her heel and rushed up the hall, breaking her way in the stream of people. She'd have to kiss the Scarecrow and the Tin Woodsman on the cheek too, but that was nothing compared to kissing Caleb.

Sydney barely kept up. "Why'd Caleb audition in the first place?" she asked.

"I have no idea, Sydney."

"You're going to get a really cute costume I bet."

"Yeah." Emma nodded.

"What do you think Mr. Baker will say?"

"What?"

"About you getting the part," Sydney pressed. "This will show him."

"Oh." Emma wrinkled her nose. "Yeah. Unless I screw up."

Sydney punched Emma lightly in the arm. "You're not going to screw up. You're going to be awesome."

"Maybe." Emma hugged her books tightly to her chest, bracing herself for failure.

TYLER should have felt guilty about what he was doing, but all he felt was pepped. He was so focused on what he was drawing he didn't see Emma and Sydney walk in, he didn't hear people congratulate Caleb about his role in the play, and he was not aware of Mr. Baker's launching into another boring lecture about Mark Twain. Tyler could only see his cartoon revenge.

It had been all Tyler had thought about since Saturday's game when they lost the city playoffs. Tyler was only in the game for the last three minutes, but they were the worst three minutes of his life. He was supposed to be a placeholder! The one reason he was in the game was because Caleb got hurt and two of their other teammates were injured. Tyler wasn't there to be a hero or anything. That would be ridiculous. There were a mere three minutes left on the clock!

But Drake had made Tyler the scapegoat. As soon as the whistle blew the vilification began. "You call that a pass?" Drake yelled. "My grandma could do better!" A lot of the other players mumbled in agreement. Caleb wasn't there to make them shut up.

Drake's dad, the coach, wasn't any help. "So close," he kept mumbling. "If only we had kept Caleb. One goal away and we would have won." Then he glared at Tyler.

Tyler's mom was honking from the car, so Tyler took one last survey of his former teammates and ran. When he got home, there was already a litany of texts waiting for him on his phone. The worst one was from Drake. "2 bad yur not yur brother," it read.

So Tyler was planning revenge. It wasn't his fault the team lost! He didn't deserve to be banished to the middle of the bus this morning on the way to school.

Caleb's betrayal was the worst. He and Drake camped out in the backseat and spread out their stuff so there was no room for Tyler to sit down. Tyler had to sit with the kindergarteners.

Revenge felt sweet. Tyler sketched his brother snuggled up in bed. Tyler drew Caleb in too-small pajamas, clutching his ratty old teddy bear and stuffed moose. *One more thing*, Tyler thought. *I need to make sure people know it's Caleb and not me.* So right under his brother's drooling expression, Tyler added the caption "CALEB FARTS HIMSELF TO SLEEP," and drew stink marks coming from the quilt. Tyler put his pen down and slid the drawing into his folder.

"Mr. Adler?" Mr. Baker asked. "Your paper?" Mr. Baker stood right next to him holding out his hand. "Your *Tom Sawyer* essay?"

Tyler swallowed hard and spit scorched his dry throat. Did Mr. Baker see what he was doing? Tyler looked into his folder and searched for his essay. But in his haste, a bunch of papers spilled to the ground. Tyler jumped out of his chair to pick them up, but Emma beat him too it. Since she sat in front of him, the papers slid under her chair. "Here," she said passing them over.

Tyler saw his essay, rumpled but present. He handed it to Mr. Baker.

"Finally," Mr. Baker grumbled.

"Um, yeah," Tyler said. But inside he was thinking, *Be sure to read it this time.*

S YDNEY didn't know lettuce could be this chewy. And macho-nachos? What was that? *Whoever designed school lunches should be locked in the cafeteria and forced to smell crud for the rest of his life.*

Sydney slid her tray on the table right next to Emma, who had been brown-bagging it ever since her lunch-line humiliation.

Sydney looked at Emma's insulated lunch bag and tried not to be jealous. It had Emma's initials on it, like her mom had ordered it from the Lands' End catalogue. *Her mom even packs a napkin,* Sydney thought. *Emma doesn't realize how lucky she is.* Sydney took a bite of what was supposed to be chips and felt her teeth squish.

Emma was angrily eating a carrot stick. "Sydney," she said, between crunches. "I need to talk to you."

"About what?" Sydney stabbed something unidentifiable with her fork.

Emma handed over Tyler's drawing. "About this. What's going on? I thought there was a truce. Don't you care about your reputation? Are you trying to get Tyler in trouble? What if you get suspended? Have you thought about that? Were you thinking at all? Were you—"

"Whoa!" Sydney held out her hands to stop the assault. Then she picked up the paper and her eyes got wide. "Whoa." *Tyler Adler,* she thought. *You're dead meat.*

"Why'd you start the cartoon war again?"

Sydney took a closer look at Caleb's farts. "I didn't." She slapped the picture down. "This wasn't me."

"Huh?"

"It wasn't me," Sydney answered. "I didn't draw this."

"Draw what?" Tiffany asked. She and Karen were approaching with their lunch trays.

"Nothing." Sydney put the picture in her pocket.

"That was mine!" Emma protested.

"Was it?" Sydney scooted over to make room for Karen and Tiffany.

Emma turned pink with annoyance. "Why are you in such a crabby mood, Sydney? Give it back!"

Sydney shook her head. "Un, uh. There's only one other person at this school who could have drawn this, and I'm going to give it to him myself."

"But I was going to give it to him!" said Emma.

"What's going on?" Karen asked.

"Who's him?" asked Tiffany.

"No one!" Sydney and Emma both said at the same time.

"So hand it over, Sydney."

"No, way. I'll give it to him myself."

"But I'm the one who took it!" Emma protested. "I should be the person who gives it back."

"But if this gets out people will think it was me."

"I won't let it get out! I'll make him trash it."

Sydney's heart raced. She felt her blood pump as she

stared her best friend down. "What if you don't, Emma? What if Ms. Elder sees it?"

"Sydney," Emma said slowly, the name rippling the air. "Don't you trust me?"

"I'm soooo confused," Karen whispered to Tiffany.

"Me too," Tiffany said.

But Sydney didn't hear them. She was still staring at Emma.

Emma held out her hand. "It's me, Sydney. I won't let you down."

Sydney wasn't so sure. *Emma will be too nice,* she thought. *She doesn't have what it takes to twist Tyler's arm hair and make him beg for mercy.*

But there was Emma with her outstretched hand. "Trust me," her best friend said. "Let me help."

Sydney agreed with her last bit of faith. "Okay." She reached into her pocket and handed Emma the cartoon.

CALEB knew it wasn't Tyler's fault the team lost last Saturday, but it wasn't like Tyler was an innocent victim either. He could've tried harder all season instead of spending so much time puking in the bathroom. Caleb felt weird every time he saw his brother. It was right before play practice and Caleb was standing onstage in the school auditorium, his nose pointed down at the ground. Tyler's sketch of Whitman Elementary was spread out in front of him.

"Good," Caleb heard somebody say. "It's you."

Caleb turned around and saw Emma in her puffy white jacket. "Dorothy," he said.

Emma blushed. "You heard."

"Of course I heard," Caleb said, wondering why Emma didn't remember their awkward discussion about the kiss.

"I need to talk to you about Caleb," Emma said.

Caleb shut his mouth real quick.

"And Sydney," Emma continued.

Caleb dropped to the ground and sat. "Yeah?" he said. "I'm all ears."

Emma sat down next to him and pulled her backpack into her lap. "Look. What you did—what you're doing with this detention, it's really great. I should have said that earlier. Thanks for not letting Sydney get in trouble for that picture of Mr. Baker."

"Of course," Caleb answered. "Mr. Baker is a jerk. He deserved it."

Emma didn't say anything. She rustled around her backpack and pulled out a piece of paper. "So why'd you do it? Were you trying to get Sydney in trouble or something?"

Oh, no. What did Tyler do this time? Caleb took the drawing out of Emma's hand and stared. *My Star Wars jammies?* he thought. *Bugger!* "What makes you think it was Ty—I mean me?"

Emma snorted. "Because it slipped off your desk."

"Sydney could've put it there."

Emma shook her head. "She didn't. Why are you denying this?"

"I'm not denying it. I'm gathering the facts."

Emma looked at Caleb with unwavering eyes. "Were you trying to frame Sydney?"

"No!" Caleb grunted. "I'd never do that to Sydney."

"Do what to me?" Sydney asked.

Caleb looked up from his spot on the floor and saw Sydney emerge from backstage holding a paintbrush.

Emma sighed loudly. "I told you, Sydney, I got this."

"I know." Sydney took a small step back. "I'm not following you or anything. I'm just here, anyway. For detention."

Caleb felt Sydney stare him down. The hairs stood up on the back of his neck. It was like being body scanned by a droid.

"Okay then," said Emma. "Let me finish talking to Tyler."

Uh, oh, Caleb thought. *Here we go.*

"Tyler!" Sydney said loudly. "That's not Tyler. That's Caleb."

"Caleb?" said another voice. Tyler, holding another

paintbrush, stepped onto the stage next to Sydney. "What are you doing here?"

"Caleb?" exclaimed Emma, jumping to her feet. "I thought you were Tyler!"

"Hey!" said Tyler. "We agreed to stop switching places!"

"Yeah?" Caleb answered, ready to snarl. "That was before you started drawing humiliating pictures of your own brother!" Caleb held out the bedtime farts sketch and crunched it up into a ball. "What was your plan? Were you going to make a hundred copies?"

"Maybe." Tyler shrugged. "Feel free to draw one of your own."

Chin, stomach, or nuts? Caleb couldn't decide what to hit first. He pushed up the sleeves of his U-Dub Huskies sweatshirt. "You asked for it, Tyler."

Sydney leapt between them. "Whoa! I get to hit Tyler first."

"No!" said Emma, shielding Tyler. "Wait! Let's talk about this."

"Talk about what?" said a loud voice. The red velvet curtain parted and there was Mr. Day holding a stack of scripts. "What's going on, people? Is there a problem?"

"No, Mr. Day," Emma answered for all of them.

But Caleb looked over at his brother and glared. As slowly as possible, Caleb held up his hand and signed the letter "t."

Then, with the other hand, Caleb made a fist and smashed it.

E MMA sat in the drama room next to Caleb. This time, she knew it was Caleb because she watched Mr. Day hand him his script. *There I go being stupid again,* Emma thought. *Is there such a thing as being face blind? Why can I never tell Caleb and Tyler apart?*

Caleb was still royally ticked off. Emma didn't need to be able to read faces to tell that. She could hear Caleb grind his teeth. "Stop that," Emma whispered. "You'll hurt your braces."

"Oh," Caleb muttered. "Sorry."

"It's going to be okay," Emma said softly. "Sydney will set him straight."

"Whatever." Caleb flipped through the pages of his script.

"Okay, people." Mr. Day started coming around with pens. "Today's called a table read. Nothing fancy. We're just reading around in a circle."

Emma's heart lurched. Read around in a circle? Even though Emma had listened to the script over and over again at home until she memorized it, she still felt like somebody had splashed cold water on her face. Emma dove into her backpack for a bookmark.

"If you want, you can highlight your lines." Mr. Day held out a basket of pens and Emma grabbed a pink highlighter.

I can do this, Emma thought. *I know this.* Reading aloud was her worst nightmare, but Emma started out fine. The first couple of minutes flew by and she tracked along perfectly. When Dorothy made her entrance, Emma was ready. Everything ran smoothly until Dorothy stepped from her farmhouse into Munchkin Land.

"That was great, Emma," Mr. Day said encouragingly. "I love your expression."

"Oh." Emma startled. "Thanks." She blushed and looked off into the distance. Then she stared down at her script and froze. Her bookmark had slid up diagonally across the page. She couldn't tell what line she was on! Emma looked back at Mr. Day, who stared at her, waiting.

The fifth grader who played Glinda didn't wait. She launched into her next line and scraped her page with marker.

"Who are the Munchkins?" Emma thought. *That's the next line.* But there's no way she could find it on her paper. *Should I say it from memory?* Emma was caught in a net of paralysis until Caleb reached over and adjusted her bookmark to the right spot. Emma smacked her hand down on the page, ready to track words again. "Who are the Munchkins?" she read, drowning the words in pink.

One scene streamed into the next and Emma knew

she wasn't alone. From the corner of her eye she saw Caleb glance over every few minutes, hounding for her bookmark. Hunting to make sure she was in the right place.

Emma kept a death grip on that bookmark. She didn't let go.

10
THE MERCURY DROPS

SYDNEY had on every fleece she owned, plus her bathrobe and fingerless gloves. She was wearing a stretched out stocking cap her mom had knit for her sixth birthday. It was a beagle with long flaps like ears that tied under her chin. Brian had on a cap from the same pattern book, only his looked like a dragon. The power was out again. This time it wasn't the pilot light—Brian triple checked. The whole neighborhood was dark. Both of them were staring at paper plates filled with mush.

Before Mrs. Taylor left for a mini-vacation to Vancouver the day before, she went to Safeway and bought a premade Thanksgiving dinner. "You're all set," she told Sydney and Brian. "There's turkey breast with all the trimmings, a tub of mashed potatoes, gravy, cranberries, and green beans. Plus there's pumpkin pie."

"You're not staying for Thanksgiving?" Brian asked.

"Don't use that tone with me, Brian. It's not like it's a big deal." Mrs. Taylor slammed the fridge door shut. "You two will be fine." A plastic grocery bag slipped off the counter onto the floor and Mrs. Taylor bent over to pick it up. When she did, her too-short sweater lifted and Sydney could see a purple butterfly inked on her mom's back.

"You got a tattoo?" Sydney freaked.

Mrs. Taylor sprang to her feet. "Yeah," she said. "A while ago." She folded over her waistband so her kids could see it better.

Brian shielded his eyes. "Yuck, Mom! I can see your underwear."

"Grow up, Brian. Mothers wear underwear too." Mrs. Taylor pulled her yoga pants back up. "It's a butterfly," she said. "I chose that because I'm a whole new person now. Beautiful, delicate, and free to fly."

It was the perfect opportunity for Sydney to be snarky. "I thought you were *driving* to Vancouver."

Mrs. Taylor's eyes narrowed. "I told you. George got a great deal on the hotel. Thanksgiving's different in Canada. Nobody there will know what day it is. I won't have to put up with any of this holiday crap."

"Why can't you bring us with you? Why can't we go too?" Sydney felt pathetic as soon as she asked.

"Because George isn't very good with kids. You know that. He doesn't even like his own."

Now that it was Thanksgiving Day Sydney and Brian were huddled in the kitchen eating frosty mashed potatoes, their mother nowhere in sight. The power had gone out in the middle of the night.

"Maybe if the gravy sits in your mouth long enough, it'll warm up and not taste so bad," Brian said.

Sydney looked at Brian and felt guilty. Brian tried so hard to make things better and Sydney was like a bloodsucking leech. She took all the goodness and hope from her brother and never gave anything back.

Sydney looked down at the pathetic paper towel she was using as a napkin. *Brian deserves better,* she thought. *Brian deserves something fancier.* Sydney knew where the china cabinet was. Sydney knew how her mom used to set the table. Why were they eating on paper plates? Sydney wished she had thought of that earlier. "I'm sorry," Sydney said.

"Sorry about what?"

"Sorry I haven't done a better job taking care of you."

"What do you mean, Sis? That's not your job."

Sydney shrugged. "Maybe it is. You always do such a good job taking care of me."

"That's different. I'm the big brother."

"The last time I checked, most big brothers don't show up at school on a two-person bike to take their sister home from detention."

Brian smiled. "It's called a tandem. And it was the perfect opportunity to fart on you."

Sydney giggled. Then she laughed even harder because it made her think about Caleb farting in his sleep.

"If you keep getting detention, we'll be in training shape by summer." Brian said. "Maybe we can enter the Seattle to Portland bike race."

"But I'd have to cut off my nose!" Sydney protested.

Brian cut her a wise-guy smile. "No big deal. You and me and Dad—we're hard core."

You and me and Dad. Sydney liked the sound of that. She lifted up her mug of water. "To Dad," she toasted.

Brian clinked his mug back. "To Dad."

They had just decided to ditch dinner and go straight to the pie when there was a knock at the front door. Sydney was too cold to remove her embarrassing beagle hat, but she did take off her bathrobe before she looked through the peep-hole.

It was Emma and her mom.

When Sydney opened the door the cold inside the house almost matched the out.

"Happy Thanksgiving!" Mrs. Silver walked in before Sydney could invite her inside.

Emma wore a puffer coat and sparkly pink boots. She

rubbed her hands over her arms to warm them up. "It's freezing in here."

"Yeah." Brian stepped into the entry way. He'd left his dragon hat in the kitchen. "The power's out on the whole block."

"Your poor mom!" Mrs. Silver tilted her head and looked into the dark living room. "Where is she? I hope her turkey isn't frozen."

"Um," Sydney answered. "She's not here right now."

"But she left us dinner," Brian added quickly.

Emma and her mom exchanged a look.

"Really?" Mrs. Silver asked. "And when is your mom supposed to be back?"

"Soon," Brian answered.

Mrs. Silver walked across the rug and stood right in front of Brian. "Define 'soon.'"

Brian's pale face became paler, making all of his pimples stand out. But he stood up tall and straight. "I'd rather not."

"Mom," Emma said with a warning tone.

Mrs. Silver looked towards the dark kitchen. Her eyes were still angry, but Sydney knew that anger wasn't for Brian.

"Go get your coats, kids," Mrs. Silver commanded. "You're coming with us to my sister's house in Edmonds."

CALEB'S home was out of power too, but the Adlers had a backup generator. It was outside on the deck humming away like there was no tomorrow. That meant two things that were absolutely essential for Thanksgiving: turkey and TV.

Only instead of watching football like normal people, the Adler television was tuned to a steady program of game shows. Grams was camped out on the sofa buried in afghans and watching *The Price is Right*. The pellet stove was on, pumping out a steady flow of heat, and the whole place was cozy.

"Happy Thanksgiving, Grams," Caleb said, sitting down. Caleb wasn't interested in *The Price is Right*, but he didn't mind spending half an hour next to Grams, pretending to like her favorite show.

"Five hundred twenty seven dollars?" Grams said to the TV. "A Frigidaire costs exactly sixty-two-dollars and thirty-one cents. I've got the receipt to prove it." Grams looked around at the couch cushions like she was searching for something. She stopped when she saw Caleb. "Walter! Is your paper route all done? You got *The PI* delivered?"

"Um, yeah," Caleb answered. But inside he was thinking, *The Seattle PI? That newspaper shut down years ago.*

"Good. People depend on you, Walter. Every job is important, no matter how small."

"Yeah." Caleb looked over at the glowing blur of the pellet stove. The red hot glare was mesmerizing. Caleb stared at it long enough that he started to remember how Thanksgiving used to be when he was little.

He could still picture Grams in her glory. The cross-stitched apron around her waist. The good smells coming from every portion of her house. Grams used to handle a double oven and a quad-burner stove. Now she could barely use a microwave.

"Do I smell turkey cooking?" Grams's question pulled Caleb back into the present.

"Yeah, Grams. It's Thanksgiving."

Grams looked at Caleb hard. A moment passed. Then another. Finally, she looked at Caleb with understanding. "Oh," she said. "It's you."

"Yeah, Grams. It's me, Caleb."

"That's right. And your brother—?"

"Tyler's in the other room, helping Mom mash the potatoes. My sister Ava's setting the table." Sometimes naming everyone really helped. Other times, telling Grams too many names just confused her further.

It all depended. Was this a good day or a bad day? That was one of the many sucky things about Alzheimer's; never knowing how things would be. Caleb's dad called Alzheimer's "the long goodbye" because it was like watching Grams go away slowly, one faded memory at a time.

"Happy Thanksgiving," Caleb said to Grams, hoping it was a good day.

Grams smiled back, the lines on her face smooshing together. "Happy Thanksgiving to you too, dear. I'm so glad to be here." She reached out and squeezed Caleb's hand. "You make things so special. I tell all my friends about you."

Caleb's heart hurt when she said that. Did Grams tell people about him or about his dad Walter?

"How's soccer going? Your dad told me you're in the playoffs."

Maybe today's going to be a good day after all, Caleb thought. *Maybe today's going to be the best day in a long time.* "Soccer. Yeah, we were in the playoffs," Caleb said. "But we lost."

"Oh. That's too bad. You were always so good with ball sports. It was how your mom potty-trained you."

"What?"

"Yes, dear. Every time you wipe your butt you should thank your mother. It took a lot of effort to teach you to do that."

"What are you talking about?" Caleb turned deep red.

Grams's blue eyes twinkled mischievously. "Your mom let you and your brother spend a week in your backyard buck naked, peeing on the grass."

"That's not true! It can't be."

"It is!" called Caleb's mom from the kitchen.

Grams nodded in agreement. "You were so desperate to play baseball, it worked. Your little potty was out there and every time you went tinkle you got to play baseball."

A faint memory of his ducky potty surfaced in Caleb's mind. "Every time you flushed the handle," Caleb whispered, "it quacked."

"Exactly!" Grams smiled. "One time when you came to my house you peed on the front lawn and scandalized the neighbors."

"I did not!"

"You did too. Or maybe it was your brother. It was hard to tell."

"That must have been before Mom started buying me boxers and Tyler briefs," Caleb said. One of the bad things about being twins was that Caleb and Tyler's clothes got mixed up. That's why their dad marked their name on every piece of clothing they owned. It was on the inside label, so nobody else could see. Plus they both wore two different types of underwear because getting that switched up would be gross. But their socks were totally communal.

"I remember how you used to run around my backyard with a football," Grams said. "You were always throwing it into the trees. I was afraid you'd hit my birdhouse."

Caleb chuckled. "One time I actually did. The whole thing fell out of the branch. I was terrified of telling you, because when I looked inside, the birdhouse was empty."

The corner of Grams's eyes crinkled up, and she laughed. "It was because it was fall. Birds don't build nests until spring. You got off easy. But you were so worried you were always really careful after that."

"You knew I hit that birdhouse and you never said anything?"

Grams shrugged. "I figured you'd learned your lesson."

"I did."

Caleb's heart filled so fast it felt like it could burst. This was the best conversation he'd had with Grams in months. It was like getting his real grandma back.

Then Tyler came in, and it all went to crap.

Grams looked at Tyler, and then she looked at Caleb. The television went to commercial and the sound cranked up.

"Walter?"

"No, Grams. It's me, Tyler."

Grams looked back at Caleb and her face clouded. Then she looked at Tyler.

"Happy Thanksgiving," Tyler said.

But Grams didn't answer. She just turned back to the television and waited for her show to come back on.

EMMA was in a snowy winterland of white. Her hands were toasty warm in mittens, and her earmuffs pinched. All around Emma, evergreens were loaded down with snow, like a forest of Christmas trees. The only thing missing was Sydney.

And maybe Brian too.

Emma stomped along the path, making wide marks with her snowshoes and thought about the night before. She didn't want to leave Sydney and Brian behind. Neither did her dad. They had argued about it, hurriedly, at her aunt's house, while Sydney and Brian played one last game of football with Emma's cousins.

"The more the merrier," Mr. Silver said. "We'll call up the lodge and reserve another room."

"Or we could get a couple of roll-aways," Emma suggested.

But Mrs. Silver refused to believe Sydney's mom wouldn't come home once she understood the situation. "No mom wants her kids to be in a cold, dark house," Mrs. Silver said. "Vancouver's only four hours away. Judy will be home before you know it."

So after they said their Thanksgiving goodbyes, Emma's family drove Sydney and Brian back home to the Taylors' house. Mr. Silver insisted on stopping at Safeway to buy several bundles of wood. Then he gave

Brian and Sydney a refresher on how to start a fire in the fireplace.

"When's the last time the flue was checked?" Mr. Silver kneeled at the brick hearth and looked up the chimney.

"The flue?" Sydney asked. "What's that?"

Mr. Silver pulled his head out. "The chimney. Has the chimney been cleaned in a while?"

Brian held a box of matches. "No. We haven't used the fireplace in forever."

"Well, I'm not sure this is a good idea then." Mr. Silver brushed off his hands. "It would probably be better—"

"It'll be fine," his wife interrupted. "Judy will be here before you know it. When I spoke to her this afternoon she said she was already in the car."

"Did she promise?" Sydney asked. "Did Mom promise to come back?"

Mrs. Silver looked at Sydney. "Well, no. She didn't promise. But she didn't have to. Your mom won't leave you kids alone in a power outage. You know that."

"So we build an A-frame, right?" Brian said, changing the subject. He was holding the biggest log from the bundle.

Emma's dad grabbed two more pieces of wood. "Yes, that's a good start. Sydney? Can you find some of those little sticks in there? We'll use those for kindling."

By the time the Silvers left, the fire crackled.

That didn't stop Emma from worrying the whole drive up to Leavenworth. How was she supposed to enjoy a faux-Bavarian village knowing her best friend might freeze to death? To make matters worse, there wasn't any cellphone reception.

After they arrived Emma's mom told her to go take a walk around the lodge and clear her head. So that's what Emma was doing. She had a bag of roasted chestnuts in her pocket that kept her hands warm.

The snow made everything peaceful. Flakes fell on Emma like white lace. She held out her tongue and the wetness melted. It was like snowshoeing through beauty.

All of a sudden, from somewhere deep inside, Emma felt the urge to write a poem. Words weren't usually her friends. But now Emma could picture a poem, just like she could picture the snowy scene in front of her. Emma could feel the words playing around in her head. Only this time, they weren't swimming. This time, the words were gently falling like snow.

Emma knew she could control those words with concentration. She could take them and make a picture. All she needed was practice.

Emma headed up the path to the hotel, anxious to find a paper and pencil. The Sleeping Lady Lodge was practically the only hotel in Leavenworth that didn't pretend to be German. Instead of oompa bands and

Bavarian bratwurst, The Sleeping Lady looked like Lincoln Logs come to life.

Snowshoeing became harder and harder. Emma looked up at the white sky and saw the snow fall faster. Thick snow melted on her sleeves. Up in front of Emma was an enormous green overcoat tromping towards her. It was Mr. Silver, ankle deep in snow.

"Emma," he called. "I was just coming to get you. There's a storm coming."

Breathless, Emma reached her father. "A storm? But it's so beautiful."

Mr. Silver held out a gloved hand and Emma grabbed it. "Yes," he said. "It is."

Emma and her dad continued up the path. They could see the door to their cabin now, with Mrs. Silver standing on the porch holding a mug of cocoa.

For some reason, Emma paused. "Dad? Do you think it's snowing in Seattle?"

"Probably not. It doesn't normally snow on Thanksgiving."

Emma stepped onto the porch and took the mug of hot chocolate from her mom. She felt the warmth permeate her mittens.

But when they entered the hot cabin, Emma shivered. Her mom had the news report on. The weatherman was predicting a snowstorm so hard that Seattle would beg for mercy.

TYLER wished his mom wasn't stuck at the hospital. Mondays weren't the same without her because it was usually his mom's day off. But there was a toxic combination of weather on all fronts. First it was snowing, then it was freezing, and now it was snowing again. Tyler's mom was stuck at Swedish Hospital delivering babies because the next shift of doctors hadn't been able to arrive. The roads were an ice rink.

At least there wasn't any school. The Seattle School District declared snow days until the roads were safe to travel.

Half the neighborhood was still out of power and the Adlers' generator rumbled out on the deck. The noise drove Tyler nuts. Between the constant hum of the generator and the incessant stream of Grams's game shows, there was nowhere to escape. Grams couldn't go back to Cascade Brooks until the weather improved.

Tyler felt guilty for being irritated with Grams, but he couldn't help it. He was in video game withdrawal.

The worst part was, things were still awful with Caleb. It got so tense the day before, that Tyler had gone out into the backyard and tried to build a snow cave so he could have some privacy. But he did something wrong because it caved in on him. He almost froze his gonads off! Now his ski coat was sopping wet and drying in front of the pellet stove. Ava complained about the smell of wet down all through breakfast.

Tyler figured Ava was really annoyed with Brian. He hadn't texted her back in days.

Between Ava's whining, Caleb's growling, and Grams's television shows, Tyler couldn't take it anymore. So after breakfast he brought an old sheet up to the room he shared with Caleb and taped it to the ceiling with duct tape. Then he cut off the extra fabric with scissors.

Now his bed on the top bunk was like his own private cabin.

Unfortunately, it was too dark. After an hour of reading books with a flashlight, Tyler got a neck cramp. So he headed downstairs to bake cookies.

Ava offered to help because there was nothing else to do.

"Okay," Tyler said, looking at the cookbook. "We don't have any chocolate chips because Caleb ate them all."

"Hey!" Caleb called from the living room. "Lay off!"

"And we don't have any peanut butter, and Dad said we couldn't use the oats because we'll need them for breakfast if we run out of milk." Tyler flipped through pages until he found the index. "So what should we make, sugar cookies or shortbread?"

Ava grabbed the cookbook and glared at her brother. "Since when did you become a cookie expert?"

"I'm not! I was just thinking about things Grams used to bake for Christmas."

"Oh." Ava pulled a strand of blonde hair behind her ear and looked thoughtful.

"How about molasses?" suggested Mr. Adler. He sat at the kitchen table, telecommuting to work. He was a web designer for Amazon.

"Snickerdoodles!" Caleb shouted from the living room. "I vote for snickerdoodles!"

"You don't get a vote!" shouted back Ava. "Not until you learn to flush the toilet!"

Tyler smiled really hard on the inside. That last turd was his.

"Let's make all of them," Ava proposed. "We'll surprise Mom."

Tyler nodded in agreement. He was just getting out the butter when they heard a knock at the front door.

Ava quickly ran her fingers through her hair and pulled down her old Stanford sweatshirt. "I look like crap."

Tyler heard the front door open and footsteps stomp in the hall. Then Brian and Sydney Taylor entered the kitchen wearing ski gear.

"Brian," Ava said, flashing her toothy smile.

What are they doing here? Tyler wondered. He tried not to gag as he watched his sister hug her boyfriend.

Caleb was considerably more hospitable. "You skied all the way here? Wow!" He reached for Sydney's jacket.

When Sydney pulled off her helmet her blonde hair looked flat. Her cheeks were flushed red from exertion, and there was an oval pressure mark across her face where the goggles had dug in.

Brian nodded to Mr. Adler, who was still sitting at the table in front of his laptop. "I'm sorry to barge in like this, but I remembered you guys had a generator. Our power's been out for five days now, and it was pretty cold. My phone's out of batteries and I couldn't text. Could we please stay here and warm up for a while?"

"Of course," Mr. Adler said. "Your mom's welcome to come here too."

Brian took off his gloves and shoved them in his pockets. "That won't be necessary."

Sydney looked down at her socks.

"Is your mom still in Vancouver?" Ava asked.

Brian nodded.

Mr. Adler shut the lid of his laptop. "You mean you two have been in your house alone since Thursday?"

"Um... no," Brian said. "We spent Thanksgiving with the Silvers. But they left for Leavenworth that night after dinner. They thought my mom was coming home."

"And she wasn't?" Mr. Adler asked.

Brian shook his head no. Sydney hooked her thumbs on the straps of her ski bib and stuck her chin out.

"You mean your mom left you alone on Thanksgiving?" Tyler asked.

Brian nodded yes and Sydney's face crumpled. Her brother put his arms around her.

"It's okay, Sydney," Caleb said, for once not calling her "Freak Show."

Ava reached over and gave Sydney a big hug. "Let me get you some dry clothes. I probably have something that fits you upstairs."

Mr. Adler cleared his throat. "I've got some things that might fit you too, Brian. Let me take a look."

"That would be great. Thanks."

Tyler looked down at the stick of butter. Suddenly, the thought of all those cookies was nauseating.

11
SNOW CAVES IN

SYDNEY felt ridiculous. She had on Ava's unicorn shirt and pink sweatpants that said "Cha-Cha Mama" on the butt.

At least her hair smelled like shampoo instead of eleven-year-old-girl-stink. This was Sydney's first shower in five days. It felt good to use soap and Ava had five different types of conditioners to choose from. Sydney finally settled on one that was supposed to smell like watermelon and kiwi. Now her hair smelled like fruit salad.

Sydney opened the bathroom door and peeked into the hall. The upstairs was cold, but not nearly as cold as Sydney's house. When she and Brian had left that morning their thermostat read forty degrees.

Sydney walked down the hallway towards the stairs.

She saw a shelf loaded with trophies. The walls were packed with so many sports pictures it was like walking through the Adler Hall of Fame. Sydney glanced through an open door into a room with brown walls and Star Wars posters. She also saw bunk beds. Her eyes got wide when she spotted a teddy bear and stuffed moose resting on the bottom bunk.

Sydney jerked her head back and headed quickly downstairs towards the sweet fragrance of cookies. She found Ava dressed in a V-neck sweater and sparkly earrings, spooning out batter.

Brian sat on a barstool, watching. He had on a flannel shirt that belonged to Mr. Adler, with the sleeves rolled up.

Sydney walked over to Brian on instinct. He pulled out a barstool for her to sit down, and smirked. "Nice unicorn shirt."

"Thanks." Sydney tried to sound like she meant it, even though she didn't.

Ava gave Sydney's outfit a swift glance. "You look so cute!"

"Thanks," Sydney mumbled again. She noticed Tyler didn't say anything. He was over at the sink washing dishes.

Right then the door from the kitchen to the garage swung open and Mr. Adler came in carrying a card table.

Caleb followed with folding chairs hanging off each arm. Brian jumped up to help close the door behind them.

"I got it." Caleb kicked the door with his foot.

"What are those for?" Sydney asked.

Mr. Adler wiped off the card table with a rag. "I thought we could get a puzzle going in the living room or maybe a game of checkers."

Checkers? Oh golly, could we? Sydney fought the urge to roll her eyes.

Tyler turned off the faucet. "Or Sydney and I could finish the set designs for the school play."

"Yeah," Sydney said. If she could get a pencil in her hand and some paper, she just might survive.

While Tyler gathered art supplies, Sydney wandered into the living room. Grams snoozed on the couch next to the blaring television.

"That's our grandma," Caleb whispered. He was opening up folding chairs carefully, so they only made small squeaks. The news on TV showed pictures of abandoned cars and snowplows. It drowned out the sound of Mr. Adler clicking open the legs of the card table and setting it up by the window.

Sydney tried to think of something to say. "I don't have any grandmas. They both died when I was little. I have a grandpa, but he lives in Maine with his new wife."

"Do you have any relatives nearby?" Mr. Adler asked.

Sydney shook her head no. "My dad was an only child. My mom's got a sister in San Diego, but that's it."

Caleb sat down by the fire. "Not a lot of cousins then, I take it."

Sydney thought of Emma's cousins from Thanksgiving, running around the backyard playing tag, and shook her head no.

Tyler came in with sketch pads and oil pastels. "Are you ready? Let's finish these things so we'll be ready for Mr. Day."

Pastels weren't Sydney's favorite medium. She wanted charcoal. But it didn't really matter. Once the page was before her, Sydney felt better. Maybe being trapped at the Adlers' house wasn't so bad after all.

Sydney only wished she wasn't wearing pink.

CALEB was stuck down on the floor, playing Solitaire. Sydney and Tyler had spread out art junk on the card table and there wasn't room for Caleb. At least he had the warm spot by the pellet stove. Caleb wondered if Sydney would be wowed by his ability to make armpit noises. It took him two years to learn. Now Caleb had the most musical pits in the whole family. "I thought you guys were done with that stuff,"

Caleb said, trying to sound casual. He hoped he could steer the conversation towards special talents.

"We are," Tyler answered. "We texted our set design to Mr. Day, but we haven't heard back yet. Now we're just messing around."

Caleb looked up at Sydney. Colors streaked down her wrists from where the oil pastels rubbed off. *Ava's going to freak out when she sees purple crayon on her shirt,* Caleb thought.

"Come join us," Tyler said, looking down at Caleb.

"Nah. I suck at art. But I can do other things." *Armpit noises, for example.*

"No," Sydney said, with a vent of frustration. "I suck. Oil pastels aren't my thing. I can never get the details right."

At that moment the grandfather clock chimed.

"Don't say 'suck,'" a stern voice said from the couch. Grams was awake and staring right at Sydney. "And keep your arms clean. If you're not careful, those colors will rub off and bleed into your project." Grams tossed the blanket aside and stood up.

Caleb held up the ace of diamonds midair. Tyler looked at Grams with wonder. Sydney wilted.

Grams walked over to the card table and bent over, inspecting Tyler and Sydney's work. She pointed to their picture of Whitman Elementary. "I like the bold use of color blocks, but the perspective on the drinking fountain is wrong." Grams tapped her finger on the offending line. "This angle, right here. It's ten degrees off."

Sydney gave Tyler an "I-told-you-so" look.

"And this," Grams said, holding out the haunted forest scene. "The Olympic Mountains! I'd recognize them anywhere. Who did this one?"

"Me," Tyler said.

Grams looked at Tyler and smiled. "Nice work, Walter. I knew you had it in you."

Sydney stared sharply at Grams.

Caleb knew what Sydney was thinking: *Is Grams crazy or what?* Would Sydney be like Emma? Would she laugh? Caleb wished he could will Grams to sit down and not embarrass herself.

But Sydney surprised him. "I did the trees," she said simply, like she wasn't fazed at all.

Caleb loosened his death grip on the ace. There Sydney went, impressing him again.

Grams held the paper closer, examining the foreground. "This hemlock looks very realistic. Your shading is excellent, but right here you pressed too hard while blending colors."

"You're right," Sydney admitted. "I'm better with pencil."

Grams put down the picture. "Interesting! Some people think pencil is harder. Do you prefer colored pencils or charcoal?"

"Both, I guess." Sydney looked at Grams with wide eyes. "You know a lot about art."

Grams smiled. "Of course I do, dear. I'm the art teacher." She turned to look at Tyler. "Walter, why don't you get us some pencils so this young lady can show us what she can do."

Tyler scrambled up from his chair and headed to his room. In his haste, he almost knocked into Mr. Adler, who was standing by the doorway.

"Class will be over in an hour," Grams said to her son. "It's not five o'clock yet."

Mr. Adler's face went white. "Mom, it's me."

But Grams ignored him. She looked looked down at Sydney. "Let's see what else you've done, dear."

Sydney's eyes were wider than ever, but she held out her papers for Grams to examine. The top portrait was a drawing of Emma.

As soon as Grams saw Emma's blue eyes and soft brown hair, she blanched. "Sonia?" Grams asked in a hushed whisper. "You drew Sonia? But I don't understand. She looks older." Grams looked at Sydney but didn't relinquish the portrait.

"Who's Sonia?" Caleb asked.

Grams stood up a little straighter. "Nobody." But she folded the picture of Emma into quarters and put it into the pocket of her tracksuit.

"I've got the pencils," Tyler said, coming back into the living room.

"Excellent, Walter." Grams pulled out a chair for Tyler. "Let's continue the lesson while we still have daylight, shall we?" Then she nodded at Caleb who was sitting down by the hearth. "You too, Walter. You too."

Caleb dropped the ace of diamonds and slid the deck of cards back together. It appeared his game of Solitaire was over.

12
THE BIG JERK TUMBLES

EMMA pressed her face against the car window and watched her dad struggle to remove snow chains from the tires. The rest stop was packed with people. Emma looked down at the ground and all she saw was slush.

Inside, Emma felt slushy too. She had that mucky gray feeling you get when you come home from vacation and have to face all your problems in the real world.

At least now they were out of the mountains and Emma could get cell phone reception. She got a couple of texts from Tiffany and Karen, but nothing from Sydney. Not even a picture! *Hopefully Sydney didn't lose her phone,* Emma thought.

That's when her mom's phone rang.

"Hello?" Mrs. Silver answered.

Emma tried to ignore it. Listening to a one-sided conversation was the most boring thing in the world.

The windows fogged up and Emma thought about writing on the glass. Maybe something easy, like her name.

"What do you mean they're not there?" Mrs. Silver said. "What do you mean you just got home?" Her voice rose. "You told me you'd be home Thursday night! Today's Tuesday! It's almost been a week!"

Emma drew out an elaborate cursive E on her window. Then she noticed her mom's vice-like grip on the phone.

"Judy, I don't understand. I told you the power was out. Your children needed you! How could you wait to leave until today?"

Emma twisted the zipper on her jacket and listened.

"Yes, but the roads were clear Thursday night and still clear Friday morning." Mrs. Silver grimaced. "I'll ask her." She turned to Emma. "Sydney and Brian aren't home. There wasn't any note. Do you have any idea where they are?"

The slushy feeling inside of Emma got slushier. She tried to think hard about where Sydney might be. "The library?" Emma suggested. "Tiffany's house? Karen's?"

Her mom conveyed those suggestions. Then she cupped her hand over the phone. "Any other ideas?"

Emma thought even harder. She remembered Sydney

and Brian alone in their cold house for Thanksgiving. She thought about melting snow, brown and yucky in the rest stop parking lot. Then she looked at her own cellphone, which didn't have any new messages from Sydney.

Emma realized what that must mean.

Sydney must be someplace horrible. Someplace too awful for pictures. Someplace Sydney would never want to go in a million years.

"Brian's girlfriend's house?" Emma suggested.

Mrs. Silver nodded and repeated that idea into her phone. Then she turned back and asked one more question. This time, her mom didn't bother covering the mouthpiece. This time, Mrs. Silver asked her question loud enough so Sydney's mom would be sure to hear. "Who's Brian's girlfriend? Judy doesn't have a clue."

SYDNEY wished Tyler would come outside to say goodbye. But he didn't. Everyone stood outside in the cold next to Mr. Adler's SUV. He had already dropped off Grams at Cascade Brooks. Now it was Sydney and Brian's turn to go home. Their skis were up top, secured in the rack.

Caleb held Sydney's poles, helmet, and goggles. "I'll see you at school tomorrow, okay?"

Sydney nodded back. She tried to ignore Brian's lingering glances with Ava.

"Well," said Mr. Adler. "Let's get this show on the road." He reached for the door handle right when an enormous vehicle barreled down the street and screeched to a halt, two wheels over the curb.

It was a gigantic, gas-guzzling Hummer. As soon as Sydney saw it, she ripped her ski poles right out of Caleb's hands.

The Hummer's passenger door swung open and two fluffy-white boots appeared. Sydney's mom climbed out, wearing tight pants and a fur coat. She looked like snow plow Barbie.

"There you are!" Mrs. Taylor exclaimed. "I've been looking for you everywhere. You had me worried sick." She tromped through the snow and threw her arm around her daughter.

Sydney didn't hug her back.

"What? No kiss for your mom?" Mrs. Taylor turned towards Brian, who had stationed himself next to Sydney.

"Where were you?" Brian asked, his voice steely.

Mrs. Taylor eyed her audience nervously. "What do you mean? I told you where I was, but I've been looking for you everywhere."

Brian's face was splotchy red. "You lied to us!"

Sydney reached out and grabbed Brian's hand. Her other hand still gripped those ski poles.

"Don't take that tone with me," Mrs. Taylor demanded. "Get in the car this instant."

"No!" Sydney said. "Never. I'd rather walk home than ride with George."

Mrs. Taylor's eyes flashed. "Right now, young lady! George and I spent the last hour driving around trying to figure out where you were. How could you be so selfish?"

Brian clenched his jaw. "No. How could you be so selfish, Mom? You left us in the cold and dark. On Thanksgiving! *For days!*"

"Don't be dramatic! It wasn't my fault the power went out." Sydney's mom said this last part to Mr. Adler. "The roads were closed. I got here as soon as I could."

That made Sydney madder. "No, you didn't! The roads were fine on Friday. You chose your big jerk boyfriend over us."

"Of course I didn't!" Mrs. Taylor said.

Mr. Adler cleared his throat. "I am curious how these two kids ended up alone for so many days in what could have been a dangerous situation."

"Dangerous?" Sydney's mom rolled her eyes. "Don't exaggerate. They were in a perfectly good house in a safe neighborhood. Brian's old enough to babysit."

"I'm not a baby!" Sydney blurted.

The Hummer honked. Mrs. Taylor turned towards the darkened windows and gave a girlish wave. "Be right there, honey!" Then she spun and glared at Mr. Adler.

"What type of parent are *you*? You keep my kids at your house and don't bother to call me? I was worried sick!"

"That's ridiculous!" Caleb shouted. "You're the one —" but he was interrupted by his dad's hand on his shoulder.

"I didn't contact you," Mr. Adler said coldly, "because all evidence indicated you had abandoned your children. You're lucky my wife wasn't home because she's a mandated reporter, required by law to call the police whenever she witnesses neglect."

Sydney's mom whipped her hair back. "I don't neglect my children!" She jumped when the Hummer honked again, grabbed Sydney's arm, and pulled her toward the car. "We're leaving right now!"

Sydney took a couple of steps. But then she heard the front door of the house slam. She looked up and saw Tyler march down the front steps. He took Sydney's helmet and goggles from Caleb and put them in their SUV. Then Tyler stood next to his brother, and the two of them eyed the Hummer with venom.

It was just the boost Sydney needed. Sydney recovered her courage and pulled her sleeve away from her mom's grasp. "No," she screamed. "I won't ride with George. He's a jerk!"

That's when there was a loud thump and heavy footsteps. "Who're you calling a jerk, missy?"

Sydney looked up at George. He was bigger and uglier

than ever. George had a long scraggly ponytail and a North Face jacket that made him puff out blue like the Abominable Snowman. "You're a jerk," Sydney declared. "A selfish butthead."

George leaned forward and yanked the ski poles from Sydney. "Get in the fracking car, missy!" He looked at Sydney's mom. "You're too soft on them, babe. I keep telling you, and you don't listen."

Sydney grabbed the ski poles back. "I won't go anywhere with you!"

Brian encircled Sydney with his arms and Caleb stepped forward, ready to bite. Tyler went with him.

"Get in the car right now!" George growled. "Or else."

"Or else what?" asked Mr. Adler, his voice rising.

"Sydney. Brian. Get in the car," their mom insisted. "We're going home."

"Not with him, we're not," Sydney popped back.

It all happened before Sydney could think. George lunged for Sydney's poles, but she swung them back out of reach. George fell forward into Brian's shoulder, in an unintentional shove that pushed Brian to the ground.

Sydney saw Brian lying in the muddy snow and flipped. She slashed at George with her ski poles, hitting him again and again with the aluminum edges until feathers flew out of his down coat.

George grasped a pole and spun Sydney around until she slammed into the grill of the Hummer.

Sydney cried out in pain and Ava screamed.

It doesn't really hurt, Sydney thought. *Not that bad at least.*

But blood flowed from a gash across Sydney's cheek. Her eyes opened wide. She watched Brian and Caleb tackle George to the ground. Tyler sprung too, protecting his brother.

Mr. Adler pulled the twins off and convinced Brian to step back. But then George leapt up and attacked Mr. Adler.

Right then the Silvers' Buick came sliding to a stop. Emma and her folks rushed out of the car. "I told you she'd be here," shouted Emma.

"Let's talk about this!" Mr. Adler yelled at George, blocking every other punch. "Fighting won't solve anything!"

Emma's dad ran in, dragged George away, and pinned his arms back, so Mr. Adler could escape.

"Your boys are thugs!" George yelled. "Just like Sydney! She's the biggest brat I know!"

"What did you say?" asked Mr. Silver. He let George go for a split second.

"Sydney and Brian both," George spit. "If they were my kids they'd get the belt."

"Mom!" Emma screamed. "Sydney's hurt!"

"George did it!" yelled Ava.

That's when Emma's dad delivered a knock-out

punch. George fell into the snow like a big blue marshmallow. "That's for my friend Bob Taylor!" said Mr. Silver, shaking out his hand.

Emma and her mom rushed to Sydney. Ava and Brian were already there, mopping up blood with their sleeves.

"For goodness' sake, Judy," Mrs. Silver exploded. "Your daughter's bleeding. Are you just going to stand there?"

Sydney heard her mom gasp out in pain, like she was the one who was wounded. "Sydney?" Mrs. Taylor squeaked. "My baby? My baby's hurt?" She came running over. "Oh my goodness," she said, cradling Sydney's head in her lap. Red streaks of blood washed over her white coat. "Mama's here now." Mrs. Taylor said. "Mama's here now and it's all going to be okay."

13
ART INSPIRES HOPE

EMMA had on her pink boots and winter coat, but she was still freezing cold. It was a week after Thanksgiving break and she stood outside of the school auditorium, waiting for her mom to pick her up. Emma stomped her feet a few times to warm up her toes and stared into the parking lot. It was nearly empty, but every once in a while a minivan or SUV pulled up and flashed its lights.

"I think we got out five minutes early," Caleb said, pulling up the hood of his purple University of Washington sweatshirt. "Normally my dad would be here already."

Emma dug her hands into her pockets. "My mom too." She and Caleb stood under a streetlight, waiting for

Tyler and Sydney to come out of the back room where they were painting scenery.

"So how do you think it's going?" Caleb asked.

Emma thought about rehearsal. Mr. Day asked them to put their scripts down and speak their lines by heart (if possible). Of course, it was super easy for Emma. But Caleb still had a long way to go. Emma smiled. "Fine. You said your lines with a lot of expression."

"I've been practicing." Caleb twisted his forehead up funny. "I can say anything I want with my eyebrows. Even swear words."

Emma laughed. "Impressive." But Emma stopped laughing when she saw a little car pull up and park by the red curb.

"Wow," Caleb said. "Cool Porsche."

"That's Sydney's mom."

"No way!"

"Yeah."

Caleb's eyebrows became tight. "So how do you think things are going? It's been over a week."

"You mean with Sydney?"

"Yeah, with Sydney."

"I'm not sure." Emma took a hand out of her pocket and twisted her hair. "I tried calling her this weekend, but she wouldn't answer. That's really not like her. My mom's been talking to Sydney's mom a lot and arranged for her to see a therapist. Apparently Mrs. Taylor broke up with

George. My mom thinks that's great, and Judy is going to shape up. But I'm worried she's just going to take it out on Sydney and Brian."

Caleb stuffed his hands in his pockets. "That wouldn't surprise me. Sydney acted funny in class today too. She stares out the window non-stop."

"Does Ava know anything? Has Brian said anything to her?"

Caleb shrugged. "I have no idea. I don't talk to my sister unless I have to."

"Oh." Emma blinked.

The backstage doors swung open and Sydney and Tyler came out. Tyler had streaks of paint marking up his fleece. But Sydney was clean and held a bundled-up smock.

"Sydney," Emma called. "Over here."

Sydney glanced at Emma and then looked out at the parking lot. "My mom's here. I better go."

"Oh. See you tomorrow." Emma waved brightly.

But Sydney didn't wave back.

"Weird," Tyler muttered, walking towards Emma and his brother.

"Exactly," Emma whispered.

Right then the twins' dad pulled up in his SUV.

"We'll wait with you, Emma, until your mom gets here," Tyler said.

"Sure," Caleb added. "It's dark out. I'll go tell Dad."

"No—wait!" Emma protested. "I'll be fine." But she was too late. Caleb had already run off to the curb.

"Emma, I have to tell you something," Tyler said.

"What?"

"It's about something strange Sydney said."

"What did she say?"

"What'd who say?" Caleb asked, trotting back.

Now it was the three of them, standing under the streetlight and freezing to death.

"Sydney," Tyler explained. "I asked her, point blank, how she was after what happened last week."

"And?" Emma asked, impressed that Tyler was so brave.

"She said, 'My mom promised to stay home more and now everything is perfect.' But Sydney didn't say it like everything was fine. She said it like things were worse than ever."

"That's what I was afraid of." Emma watched her mom's car pull into the lot. "Would you keep trying, Tyler? Tomorrow when you're painting scenes, would you talk to Sydney again?"

Tyler shook his head. "She's not going to be there. We're all done with the sets."

"Oh," Emma said. "Congratulations."

"See?" Tyler said. "That's how Sydney said it too. Like she wasn't happy about it at all."

SYDNEY and Brian had gone from no supervision to their mom trying to make up for things on overdrive. Picking Sydney up from detention yesterday was just the beginning. When Mrs. Taylor wasn't paying bills, calling the furnace guy, or mopping the floor in a full-on cleaning rampage, she was talking on the phone with Emma's mom for hours. Then she'd hang up and go into Sydney's room, all weepy. "You're my top priority," she'd sob. "You and Brian. I'm so sorry I lost sight of that this year." Mrs. Taylor had been seeing her therapist twice a week and wanted Sydney and Brian to come too.

When Sydney walked home from the school bus stop Tuesday afternoon she found her mom waiting in the kitchen holding car keys and a journal. "Great! You're here," Mrs. Taylor said. She shoved the book into Sydney's hands before Sydney had the chance to put down her backpack. "I bought this diary for you so you could express all of your feelings. Dr. Victoria says it's important to analyze your emotions. You shouldn't keep them bottled up or they'll explode."

Sydney dropped the journal onto the countertop like it was burning coal. Then she stomped over to the refrigerator and swung the door open. Kale, chia seeds, Greek yogurt and figs—the fridge was packed with everything except something decent to eat. Sydney grabbed a package of cheese curds and screwed up her nose.

"Good idea," said her mom. "Grab a snack and let's go. Dr. Victoria can't wait to meet you! I've told her all about everything." Mrs. Taylor slid into a black leather jacket and hooked her purse over her shoulder.

Sydney stood in front of the fridge and let icy air blast her face. She shifted underneath the weight of her backpack and coat, but she didn't take them off.

"Well?" demanded Mrs. Taylor. "What are you waiting for?"

Sydney slammed the door shut so hard the refrigerator magnets rattled. "I'm not going anywhere with you! And you can't make me."

"But Dr. Victoria says—"

"I don't care what she says! And I don't care what you say either." Sydney crammed the package of cheese into her backpack. Then she rifled through the kitchen cabinet for a juice box.

Mrs. Taylor tried a different approach. "Things have been rough recently and I know I've been distracted but—"

"Distracted? No buts, Mom." Sydney's face turned purple with rage. *"I hate you!"*

Mrs. Taylor's chin trembled. "Sydney!" Her voice quavered. "You get in the car right now, young lady, and we'll talk about this with Dr. Victoria. You're not allowed to sass me like that."

"No, Mom. *You're* not allowed. You don't get to tell me what to do."

"Of course I do. I'm your mother!"

"Mothers don't leave their children on Thanksgiving. They don't choose their stupid jerk boyfriends over their kids. They don't get butterfly tattoos next to their butt cracks!"

Mrs. Taylor's gripped her car keys with white knuckles. "In the car. Right now."

"No!" Sydney swiped the journal off the counter and hurled it across the room. "Never! And if you ever abandon me or my brother again I'll tell Emma's mom. And Mr. Day. And Ms. Elder. And the police. I'll call the president if I have to!" Sydney yelled so violently it felt like an earthquake emanated from her stomach. She didn't hear the front door open. It wasn't until Brian stood right next to her elbow that she realized her brother was home from school too.

Tears coursed down Sydney's cheeks when she felt Brian beside her. His presence was enough to make her lower her voice. "Brian deserves better," Sydney whispered. "Brian deserves more."

Brian placed a cool hand on Sydney's shoulder and she let him for a moment. But then Sydney shrugged him off and flew out of the house. When she saw her scooter on the front porch, she hopped on, despite the fact that her helmet was in the garage.

It felt good to pound the pavement with her foot. It felt swell when the wind rushed over her blonde hair. For the first few blocks Sydney rolled in a blaze of hurt. All she saw was white hot rage. But then Sydney remembered the art supplies in her backpack. She pictured the one moment in the past few weeks when she was truly happy. Thinking about that moment gave her a purpose. Sydney decided to find Tyler's grandma.

Twenty minutes later Sydney stood in front of a sign that read, "Cascade Brooks: The premier retirement home for loved ones with mild memory impairment." *Will Tyler and Caleb's grandma remember me?* Sydney wondered.

She stashed her scooter behind a rhododendron and hoped it stayed hidden. If somebody stole her scooter it would be a long walk home. It was getting dark out—and scary. But at that point, Sydney didn't really care. There was nothing outside in the world as terrible as the hurt she felt inside.

Sydney pushed open the door to Cascade Brooks and walked into the lobby. Coming from the noise, dirt, and biting cold of the city, the quietness was jarring. A fake fire burned on the hearth and synthesized music played. The whole place was decorated for Christmas.

Sydney saw a four-foot artificial snowman and considered fleeing. Those beady eyes made everything seem bleak. *This was a bad idea,* Sydney thought. *I should go home right now.*

But she didn't.

"Can I help you?" asked the receptionist. She was a middle-aged woman wearing an ugly Christmas sweater. She eyed Sydney's army jacket and ripped jeans with suspicion. Sydney's spiked bracelet probably didn't help.

"Um," Sydney stammered. "I'm here to see Mrs. Adler. Could you please tell me which room?"

The receptionist squinted at Sydney. "Oh. Let me check the list." She clicked on the computer for a few seconds before looking up again. "And your name is?"

"Sydney Taylor."

"Got it. I'll be right back." The receptionist stepped away to a back room, her jingle bell necklace ringing.

Sydney looked around the lobby again and saw a gigantic tub of hand sanitizer. "Cleanliness saves lives," the sign read. "Protecting our vulnerable residents is our number one goal." Sydney pumped out a bunch of squirts and rubbed her hands together until her nose burned from the smell of alcohol.

"Right-oh," the receptionist said, returning. "Mrs. Adler is in room 305. Take the elevator to the right."

"Great. Thanks." Sydney walked quickly away, anxious to leave the creepy snowman behind.

The ride up the elevator was silent. A sign posted inside advertised Bridge Club followed by a prime rib dinner. Sydney braced herself when the doors slid open. But she didn't see anybody, not even an old guy in a wheelchair.

Sydney walked down the hallway until she got to room 305. Right by the number was a drawing of a kitty cat.

I can do this, Sydney thought. *I just hope she says yes.*

It only took a couple of knocks before the door swung wide open. Grams stood there in a track suit and slippers. Her gray hair was pulled back into a messy bun, with a pencil sticking out.

"Hello," she said to Sydney. "You're late."

"I am? I'm sorry. I didn't know you were expecting me."

"Of course I was," said Grams. "You better come in."

"Oh." Sydney walked into the tiny room. It was so warm and cozy it was like entering a hug. There were candy jars everywhere and a velvet green couch.

"Did you bring your supplies?"

"What?" Sydney asked. "Um, yeah. I did."

"Don't say 'yeah.' It's sloppy. Being an artist is no excuse for slip-shod diction."

"No. Of course not," Sydney stammered. Then she plowed ahead with what she came to ask. "Mrs. Adler. It's me, Sydney Taylor. I met you at Tyler and Caleb's house the other weekend. I was wondering if you would be willing to give me some more art lessons."

"Of course I know who you are. We always begin at four o'clock. Let me make the tea and then we'll get started." Grams took a few steps over to her tiny kitchen. Really it was just a counter with a miniscule refrigerator and microwave.

"So 'yes' then? You'll give me lessons?"

"I've given you lessons all year, haven't I?" Grams opened up a box of Earl Gray. "Are you okay with caffeine? Or would you like something herbal?"

"Whatever you have is fine," Sydney answered. "But, Mrs. Adler, you haven't given me lessons before. I'm—I'm a new student."

Grams closed the microwave door and peered at the buttons. "This is the confusing part. This oven never works right."

"Mrs. Adler?" Sydney asked. "We haven't had lessons before."

"That's okay, dear," Grams said, still staring at the microwave. "We can start today. Four o'clock like usual. As soon as I make the tea."

Sydney felt flooded with relief. "Great. Thank you!" She took a step forward and looked at the microwave panel. "This button right here, Mrs. Adler. It said 'cook for one minute.' Let's press it twice."

Grams held up her hand and Sydney helped her press the button.

"You're so clever, dear," Grams said. "I remember."

But then she smiled. "Except with oil pastels. Am I right?"

"Yeah—I mean yes. That's why I need your help."

"You've come to the right place." Grams opened up a box of cookies.

Yeah, Sydney thought. *Maybe I have.*

TYLER felt weird visiting Grams without Caleb. But that morning when Tyler woke up, Caleb wasn't there. When Tyler came down to breakfast his dad said Ava was at the library and Caleb was at Drake's basketball game.

"Basketball?" Tyler asked. "Oh, yeah. I guess the season started." *Another thing I suck at,* Tyler thought. *But why didn't Caleb try out for the team?*

"Mom's at the hospital, so it's just you and me with Grams this morning," Mr. Adler said.

"Okay."

"Bring your sketchpad," Mr. Adler added. "I'm hoping she's up for some art."

It was a wish that got fulfilled.

When Grams opened the door to her apartment Tyler immediately perked up. He saw art everywhere. A clothesline strung across the room held water colors, drying. A girl on a bicycle. A red brick house. A pod of orcas. The Edmonds ferry sailing off into Puget Sound. The Space Needle rising into the sun. It was like an art explosion, right there in her living room.

"Oh," Grams said. "Hello." She wore a smock and had a paintbrush stuck behind her ear.

Tyler gave Grams a big hug and so did his dad. Grams stepped back a little, like she was startled by the affection. "You might as well come in," she said. "But I was in the middle of something." She indicated an easel in the corner with the faint outline of a face. All Tyler could see was a hairline and blue eyes.

"Mom," Mr. Adler said as he walked into the room. "You've started painting again! I knew you still had it in you."

"Of course I have it in me. Whatever do you mean?"

"It's been so long," Tyler said. "I haven't seen you paint in over a year. This is awesome."

"'Awesome?'" Grams shrugged. "I don't know about that. But yes, the muse has struck again and I am compelled to answer her call."

Tyler walked forward to the clothesline and looked at a picture of a squirrel resting on a branch of a cedar tree. "Is this the tree outside your window?"

Grams nodded. "That's the one. There's always a flurry of squirrels outside. Did you know that's what they're called? A flurry of squirrels."

"Yes," said Tyler. "It's called venery. Weird groupings of animals. You taught me that."

Grams's eyes went wide. "I did? But I don't know you."

Tyler's heart jerked. "You don't?"

Grams shook her head.

"Oh," said Tyler slowly. "My mistake. My name's Tyler. Nice to meet you." Tyler looked back at the squirrel picture. The fineness of detail was impressive. You could almost see the rodent wiggle its nose. Then he turned to Grams. "My grandma taught me about venery. She loves vocabulary almost as much as I do. A flurry of squirrels, a murder of crows, a—"

"Cloud of starlings, a herd of wrens," said Tyler's dad softly.

"A descent of woodpeckers," added Tyler. "A gam of whales, a knot of toads, a hover of trout."

"An ambush of tigers," said Grams. "A gang of turkeys, a pitying of turtle doves. All those names come from the middle ages."

"You remember a lot," whispered Mr. Adler. "But do you remember me?"

"No, dear. I'm sorry. Have we met?"

Mr. Adler turned away and looked out the window.

"Dad," Tyler said. "Take a look at this." Tyler stared at a painting of a young mother holding an infant. The woman had soft blue eyes and was letting the baby grasp her finger in his tiny fist. "Is that you, Dad?"

"No," Grams corrected, gently. "That's my son Walter. He's such a good baby. He never cries. Not even when I'm teaching one of my classes."

Tyler's stomach lurched. The feelings inside him percolated into something sick.

"Are you here for a class?" Grams asked. "You're early. It's not four o'clock yet."

Tyler pointed to his dad. "Grams, this is Walter. Your son."

Grams nodded. "Of course, dear. Of course. And you are—?"

"I'm your grandson, Tyler." Tyler held up his sketchpad. "I like art too."

"Wonderful, dear. But you're early. It's not four o'clock yet."

Mr. Adler cleared his throat. "I'm so sorry, Mrs. Adler. Please forgive the intrusion." His voice was steeped with politeness.

Tyler smelled the hurt. "Could we stay and visit awhile, Grams?"

Grams shook her head. "I'm sorry, but I'm very busy."

"Could you tell us more about your son?" Tyler asked.

"About Walter?"

That got Grams's attention. She sank down into the couch and pulled a picture out of her pocket. "Of course, dear. Of course." She caressed the photograph with her hand. "He's a bundle of energy."

Tyler couldn't see the image, but he could tell the picture was wrinkled, like it had been kept in Grams's pocket for years. He sat down on one side of Grams, and his dad sat on the other.

"Walter learned the whole alphabet by the time he was two." Grams looked at Tyler and then at Mr. Adler. "You probably think I'm bragging, but I'm not. It's the truth. Walter was reading by the time he was four years old. Such a smart little boy."

Tyler's dad swallowed hard. "You sound very proud of him, Mrs. Adler."

Grams tilted her head and smiled. "I am. He's something special." Then she reached out her hand and uncovered his picture. "And so cute too."

When Tyler saw the picture he started to shake. He folded his arms to keep his torso still.

Tyler was looking at a kindergarten picture of himself.

Or maybe Caleb. Tyler couldn't tell for sure.

"A darling boy. Absolutely darling," Mr. Adler said. "Mother? I mean, Mrs. Adler? Are you happy here, in this apartment?"

"The light is sub-par. Is that what you mean?"

"No," Mr. Adler said. "Not exactly."

We just want what's best for you, Tyler thought. *We want you to be safe.*

Even if it meant moving to another place within Cascade Brooks. Even if it meant moving to the Alzheimer's ward.

CALEB was on the lower bunk looking up at stuff he was supposed to memorize for *The Wizard of Oz*. It was Saturday night and Caleb had plastered his script all over the place, so it was the first thing he saw when he woke up in the morning and the last thing when he went to sleep. He hoped to memorize his lines through osmosis.

"'I didn't bite him!'" Caleb exclaimed.

"What?" Tyler opened up the curtains surrounding his top bunk and leaned his head down. "Did you say something?"

"Nah. I was just practicing for the play. Sorry." Caleb propped himself up on his elbows so he could get a better look at his lines.

"Oh. No biggie." Tyler retreated to his cubbyhole and closed the curtains.

It had been a lot better between the twins ever since that day they tackled George into the snow. Things weren't perfect, but it was a start. Caleb stared upward. This memorization stuff was so hard Caleb's brain hurt. But then he got an idea that could solve everything.

"Tyler? Now that the scenery is all done, maybe you could join the cast. You could be my understudy."

"Man, that would be fun, but this is your thing, not mine."

"What's that supposed to mean?" Caleb asked. "You were involved with the play before me. You're the whole reason I auditioned!"

"Huh?" Tyler leaned down again. "What do you mean you auditioned because of me?"

Caleb grabbed a LEGO mini figure and popped off the head. "You and me, Tyler. That's how we roll. I do soccer, you do soccer. You do a play, I do a play. Double the power. Double the awesome." Caleb popped the head back on.

"No, Caleb. Not anymore."

"Huh?"

Tyler flipped down from the top bunk and landed squarely on Caleb's mattress.

"Hey," said Caleb. "Watch out!"

Tyler leaned against the wall. "Sorry."

"What do you mean 'not anymore'?"

"Because I'm done."

Caleb felt something cold and sinister flow over him, like an icy cold breeze.

"You and me, Caleb, we're two different people."

"Yeah, so?"

"We have different interests. Different talents."

"Of course we do. So what?"

"So we should be different," Tyler blurted out. "Do different things. Wear different socks!"

"What? What does this have to do with socks?"

"Doesn't it bother you Mom buys us the same socks? I never know which socks are yours and which are mine. It's so gross. Our sweat gets mixed up."

"What's the big deal?" Caleb protested. "It's not like Mom buys us the same underwear."

"That's even worse!" Tyler exploded. "I hate briefs! Why do I have to be the one who wears briefs? Why can't I wear boxers? Or boxer-briefs? Or why can't we just buy different colors?"

"Whoa. That's a lot of anger about underwear. You can be the boxer person from now on. Starting tomorrow, we'll trade."

"I don't want to trade! I don't want your underwear! That's gross!"

"Okay then. We'll buy new underwear. Whatever." Caleb flicked the mini figure across the room. But then the horrible truth occurred to him. *This isn't about underwear*, he thought. *This is about Tyler wishing he wasn't a twin.*

"This isn't about underwear," Tyler said, as if reading Caleb's mind.

"I know it isn't. So why don't you go up to your cave and leave me alone?"

"Dude," Tyler said.

But Caleb didn't answer. He rolled over and faced the wall.

"We can still be the same and be different, both at the same time," Tyler said. "Double the power, double the awesome. Right?"

Caleb rolled back to look at his brother. For a moment he didn't answer.

"Right?" Tyler asked again. "If we learn to do different things, we'll have twice as much power." He held up a sign language "c" and waited.

"Twice as much power," Caleb answered. He considered this for a moment. "Yeah, maybe." Slowly, Caleb signed the letter "t" and smiled.

14
SOMETHING'S SERIOUSLY WRONG

SYDNEY thought this was the best Monday ever. At least, it was the best Monday in a long time. She didn't care that Christmas was only twelve days away. Normally this time of year was super hard for Sydney. Holidays without her dad were awful. But this December was different. This Monday was special because for the first time, in a long time, Sydney had somebody waiting for her when she got out of school. A hot cup of tea and a plate of cookies. Was that too much to ask?

Not from Grams it wasn't.

By the time Sydney biked from school to Cascade Brooks it was four o'clock on the dot. She stood at the threshold of apartment 305 and didn't need to knock. Grams was right there waiting, holding open the door.

"You're here!" Grams said brightly. "Let me get your coat."

"Thank you, Mrs. Adler." Sydney stepped into the warmth and let it envelop her like a hug. "I brought some more paint and new brushes."

"Excellent." Grams indicated a plate of store-bought cookies on the coffee table. "I'm just waiting on the tea. It's in the box right now."

Sydney looked over at the tiny kitchen. The microwave was dark and quiet. "You mean the microwave? Did you press the button?"

"The button?"

"The one I put the star sticker on?" Sydney dropped her backpack and walked to the kitchen. "Never mind, Mrs. Adler. I'll do it. This microwave is tricky."

"Exactly, dear. That's what I keep saying, but nobody listens."

Saying to who? Sydney wondered, but she didn't ask. Sydney nuked the tea and waited for the beep. Then she dumped the bags in the trash and tested the temperature to make sure the tea wasn't too hot for Grams.

"Here we go, Mrs. Adler. All ready for class." Sydney set the tea on the coffee table and took her art supplies out of her backpack

"Excellent, dear, excellent." Grams was already sitting on the couch with an art book resting on her knees. "I've been waiting for you to come all day. I've got a good lesson for this afternoon, but it's a hard one. Are you up for a challenge?"

"I was born ready," Sydney answered. She took off her spiked leather bracelet and put it in her backpack. Sydney didn't want to risk poking a hole in her work.

"Good," Grams said. "But don't say I didn't warn you. Today's lesson is about darkness."

"What?" Sydney asked.

"Darkness. We're coming up to the winter solstice, the darkest day of the year. I always teach the same lesson this time of year."

"So what is it? What's the lesson?"

"It's about *chiaroscuro*. That means using light and dark in artwork to produce special effects." Grams opened her book and showed Sydney some examples. "The best artists know how to master shadows. They shade things up or down, they express hope or sadness, they make people feel something genuine with one tiny stroke of a brush."

When Sydney looked at the pictures tiny hairs on her arms stood up. She thought about what Mr. Day said about art having the power to squeeze people's hearts and make them think. It reminded her how he said she had the choice to either light a candle or rage against the dark.

"Today, dear, we'll practice chiaroscuro by drawing the darkest day of our life."

"You mean dark, like the middle of the night?"

"No, dear. I mean sadness. It won't be easy. But I've seen your work, and I know you're ready." Grams looked up at the squirrel picture hanging off the clothesline. "If you can paint that little nutter up there, then you're ready for harder things."

"Yeah," said Sydney. "I mean yes—I mean are you sure?"

Grams smiled kindly and nodded. She put down the book and picked up some supplies from the coffee table. "I think I'm ready too."

Sydney gulped. Her own pencil felt heavy in her hand.

"Do you need a moment to think, dear? Or do you know what to draw?"

"I know," said Sydney. "I know." She bent her head low and let the pain flow out.

First she drew the lake. It was greenish in hue, and the sun reflected over part of the water in a brilliant blaze of light. The other part of the lake was dark, where the shadows fell from trees and ducks glided out in the water.

There was a patchwork quilt on the grass, protecting everyone from duck poop. It had flowers and leaves and some sort of Scandinavian design.

Next Sydney drew Emma, sitting crisscross-applesauce and holding a sandwich. Nine-year-old Emma was easy to draw. Her blue eyes, her curling brown hair, her pink sundress; Sydney let every detail run through her pencil.

Emma's mom was a lot like Emma, only bigger and softer and with a few wispy gray hairs at her temple. She wore mom-jeans and sandals. Her short-sleeve shirt had a triangle and a hooked letter on it. Emma said it was from her mom's college sorority, Delta Gamma.

Sydney drew herself lying on the blanket staring up at the clouds. Her arms were spread wide, like she was making a snow angel in summer. She wore a sundress too. It was purple, ruffled, and beautiful. Her white blonde hair framed her face like a cloud.

Chiaroscuro, Sydney remembered. The contrast of light and dark. So she took the darker colors and filled in shade from the tree, speckling the blanket, and making parts of the picture unclear.

But one spot of the picture was perfectly vivid.

In the center of the quilt, like a ticking time-bomb, was a cell phone.

Sydney's saddest day ever was her last moment of peace before somebody called to tell her the news.

Sydney's dad was gone. His car smashed up. And Sydney's mom had turned the corner into despair.

A few tiny strokes of pencil and all that pain was on paper.

"Sonia," Grams whispered, looking over Sydney's shoulder.

"What?"

"You drew Sonia too."

"Huh?" Sydney grabbed her pencil like a sword. "What?"

"My picture," Grams said, "is right after Sonia drowned."

Grams held up paper and Sydney felt slain.

It's Emma. Sydney thought. *It's Emma floating in water, tangled up in seaweed.*

TYLER warmed up with a hot cup of chocolate. His dad packed a thermos for all three kids, and Tyler nursed his all morning, although you weren't supposed to drink in class. But they had a substitute today, who was clueless. They weren't even at their assigned seats.

"Tyler," whispered Sydney. "I need to talk to you. It's important."

"What?" Tyler almost knocked over his thermos. Sydney came sneaking up from nowhere. "What's the matter?" He looked at Sydney and noticed the dark circles under her eyes. Her hair was colorless, like she'd washed the marker out. Sydney's t-shirt looked old and ratty. She wore a brown sweatshirt with "Brian Taylor" written across the top.

Call it intuition. Call it empathy. Call it whatever. Tyler scooted his desk closer to Sydney and rearranged his math book.

"What's going on?" Tyler asked.

"Shhh!" Karen whispered. "We're supposed to be working on this problem set. It might be on the test."

"Bug off, Karen. We're working in a small group." Tyler looked back at Sydney. "What's the matter?"

Sydney sniffed really hard. "It's about..."

"About what?" Tyler whispered. He gave Emma's seat a quick glance, but it was empty. Emma hadn't come back from Miss Klimey's yet. Caleb was off in the corner playing tic-tac-toe with Drake. "Are you okay?"

Sydney shook her head and wiped her eyes on the back of her sleeve.

"Are you crying?" Tyler asked, a bit louder.

"Shhh!" Karen hushed.

"Is there a problem?" the substitute asked from up front by the whiteboard.

Tyler said the first thing that came to his mind. "Sydney's going to puke!" Then he grabbed her elbow and pulled her out of her chair. The desks in front of them parted like the Red Sea. Tyler and Sydney were out in the hallway before they knew it.

Sydney jerked her elbow away. "Great. Now everyone thinks I'm barfing." She pulled up the hood of her sweatshirt and walked away.

"Wait!" Tyler called after her. "Hold on a minute." He followed her steps briskly. When she didn't stop he ran and hopped in front of her. "What's the matter? Is it your mom? Is it her boyfriend? Are things okay?"

"My mom's not dating George anymore. He dumped her. He said Brian and I were too much drama."

"Oh. That's a good thing—I guess."

"I guess."

"So is that what you wanted to talk to me about?"

"No," Sydney muttered. "It wasn't." But she didn't elaborate.

"So what is it?"

"Nothing. I shouldn't have said anything. Look, I'll go to the nurse's office and have them look down my throat or something and then I'll come back to class like everything is fine. Like I didn't puke after all."

"But it's not fine," said Tyler. "I can tell."

Tyler felt Sydney's eyes cross his face like the scanner at the grocery store reading a barcode.

Only for some reason, the help Tyler wanted to offer didn't register.

"Nothing's fine," Sydney said. "That's life."

"No," Tyler said as Sydney walked away. "It doesn't have to be that way. Sydney, come back!"

But she didn't.

EMMA stared at the yellow light in the cafeteria that meant it was too loud and everyone was supposed to use quiet voices. The lunch ladies patrolled the aisles like vultures.

"What's with all the brown?" Tiffany asked Sydney.

Emma was wondering about that too but hadn't said anything because Sydney was always so sensitive about her wardrobe.

Sydney wore ratty brown corduroys, an old shirt, and a baseball sweatshirt that said The Brown Bombers. *It's like she dug around Brian's hand-me-downs*, Emma thought. *What's going on now?*

Sydney stuck her chin out. "I like brown. Color is overrated." She ripped off a bite of her grilled cheese sandwich and chomped away.

Emma nibbled her peanut butter and jelly. She wished her mom had packed enough Christmas cookies to share. She considered splitting the gingerbread in two so that she, Sydney, Karen, and Tiffany could each eat half a person. But that seemed like gingerbread murder.

"How's the play going?" Karen asked.

Emma wiped her mouth with her snowman napkin. "Great. Mr. Day is teaching us about blocking, which means where we're supposed to stand and stuff."

"Are you really going to have to kiss Caleb?" Tiffany looked over to the table where the twins sat and giggled.

Emma looked over too. Caleb was blowing straw wrappers and Tyler batted them away with his hands.

Tyler turned and caught Emma's eyes. Then he looked pointedly at Sydney.

Emma looked at Sydney too. Her best friend was slumped over her lunch tray jamming carrot sticks in her mouth.

Something is definitely wrong, Emma thought.

"Hello? Emma?" Tiffany asked. "Are you lost in thought about kissing Caleb?"

"What?" Emma startled. "No! Of course not." Emma crumpled her napkin. "I don't have to really kiss him anyway. I only have to peck him on the cheek. Plus I have to kiss the two fifth graders that play the Scarecrow and the Tin Woodsman."

"Oh," Karen said. "Yikes! When's the play again?"

"Not until February. Around Valentine's Day," Emma answered. "But the background scenery is already painted, thanks to Sydney and Tyler. You should see it. It's amazing."

"Can't wait," said Karen. Tiffany nodded too.

Sydney didn't respond.

"Tyler's working on the cover design for the program," Emma said to Sydney. "Mr. Day said he asked you for input too, but you never got back to him."

"The whole thing is stupid," muttered Sydney.

Emma turned pink. "What do you mean? It's not

stupid. The play's going to be amazing. Why would you say that?"

"Not you!" Sydney looked up quickly. "I didn't mean you being Dorothy. I only meant the idea of school plays in general is stupid."

"What's that supposed to mean, Sydney?" Emma asked, her voice rising. From the corner of her eye she saw Tyler look across the room at them.

"Why do extra school stuff when you don't have to?" Sydney said. "Why not just go home and be yourself?"

"But what about college?" protested Karen. "Extra work gets you into college. Being yourself doesn't."

"That's baloney," said Sydney. "And if it was true, why would I want to go to a college that didn't care about the real me?"

Emma tried to understand her best friend, but it was hard. "I care about the real you, Sydney. And I care about the play too. Some things are worth doing because they're important. Like school and plays."

"And piano lessons," said Karen.

"And the possibility of kissing Caleb," Tiffany offered.

"Yeah," Emma agreed. Then her head flicked. "No!"

Sydney threw her lunch litter on her tray and prepared to leave for recess. "Look, guys. You and me. We're different. You can go ahead with all of your stupid sixth-grade stuff and have a grand old time. But I'm done with that." Sydney stood up from the table and stalked away.

"Sydney, wait!" Emma called.

"What's got into her? Tiffany asked.

"I don't know," said Emma. "But I'm going to find out."

CALEB and Drake shot hoops and played Horse all recess. Only instead of calling it "Horse" they renamed the game "Poop." It was so much better that way. Drake had been stuck on P-O-O for ten minutes now, but Caleb was still on P.

Usually Tyler played with them too, but today he was across the blacktop playing chess with one of the fifth graders. For the first time in a long time, Caleb was okay with that. *The same, but different,* he thought.

When Drake stepped up to make a shot, Caleb chanted, "Poo! Poo! Poo!"

Drake squinted his eyes and made the perfect shot. "Beat that, Caleb!" Drake stepped aside for him to claim his spot and then slammed the ball into Caleb's middle.

"Ugh," Caleb gasped. Then he made a jump shot. The ball hit net and made a clean swoosh to the ground. "I could P all my life," Caleb bragged.

"Lucky shot, P-boy," Drake grinned. "You should have joined the team."

"I'm taking the year off. Tyler and I are snowboarding

this winter." *Something fun we can do together,* Caleb thought. *Something we both still enjoy.*

"But you're missing basketball! You're crazy!"

"That's what they tell me," Caleb said, wrinkling his eyebrows funny.

"Speaking of crazy, look at Freak Show over there. Maybe we should call her Brown Town." Drake dribbled the ball and nodded to the corner of the field.

Caleb looked across the playground and saw Sydney in head-to-toe brown, heading into the girls' restroom. Emma waited outside.

"She looks like a brown turd," Drake said. Then he shot the ball and missed.

Caleb grinned wide, showing all his teeth. "Takes one to know one, Mr. Poop." Then he raced off across the distance to talk to Emma. He was sweaty by the time he reached her.

"Caleb!" Emma said. "Your grandma—I mean—"

"What?" Caleb wiped off his forehead with his UW sweatshirt.

Emma took a step back and turned her nose into the fresh air. "Nothing," she said. "I don't know anything—I mean—Your grandma—I mean—have you been playing hard?" Emma's chin quivered.

Why is Emma rambling? Caleb wondered. "Yeah," he answered. "I kicked Drake's butt in basketball."

Caleb walked over to the drinking fountain for some

water, careful not to let his tongue touch metal. It was freezing, even though it was sunny. Caleb lapped up some water and turned back to Emma. "I need to ask you a favor."

"Sure," Emma said. "Anything."

"Would you help me learn my lines for the play? You have the whole thing memorized and I can barely manage one part."

"Oh," Emma said, blushing. "That's nothing. It's not that hard."

"But it *is* that hard, Emma. You're really smart to be able to do that."

Emma turned pinker. "No, it's no big deal. I just listened to it on CD. That's my trick."

"On CD?"

"Yeah," Emma said. "Or maybe you might like to watch the movie over and over. I bet you have some commercials memorized, right?"

"Yeah, so?"

"So, it's the same thing," said Emma. "Watch *The Wizard of Oz* on repeat until you've got it."

"Watch what?" Sydney asked, coming out of the bathroom. She looked hard at Caleb's forehead. "PU, Caleb. You stink."

Caleb sniffed his pits. "Oh," he said. "Sorry. We had PE this morning. Remember?"

Sydney shrugged. "Whatever." Then she walked away.

"Sydney, wait!" Emma called. "We need to talk! Come back!" Emma ran off without saying goodbye.

Caleb waved. "Bye."

"What was that all about?" Tyler asked, walking up. "Did Sydney seem weird to you?"

"No" Caleb said. "But Emma did."

"Girls are so bizarre."

"Don't I know it," Caleb answered. "I'm thankful I'm a guy every time I pee standing up."

TYLER walked down the hall of Whitman Elementary and heard somebody sing the *Jingle Bells* song about how Batman smells. It was the Friday before winter vacation and the jubilation was palatable.

The kindergarteners decorated school with pink and red poinsettias made out of construction paper. The primary grades made snowmen out of craft sticks and cotton balls. The sixth graders didn't get to do anything fun like that, but Mr. Baker did let them watch a movie version of Charles Dickens' *A Christmas Carol*.

Before Tyler and Caleb left for school that morning, their dad handed over a Starbucks gift card that was supposed to be Mr. Baker's teacher present.

"No way am I giving that guy anything," Caleb said.

So it was all up to Tyler, even though he detested being a messenger boy almost as much as he hated Mr. Baker. Why couldn't his dad have dropped the card off himself? Tyler figured he'd give the card to the school secretary and let her deal with it. That's where he was headed in the middle of second recess when Emma stopped him.

"Caleb, wait! I need talk to you. It's important."

Tyler spun around. *Something important?* For a half second Tyler thought of answering as Caleb, but then he dismissed the idea. *Caleb and I made a pact,* he thought. *No more switching places, especially with girls.*

"It's me, Emma. Tyler."

"Oh." Emma paused on the linoleum and stuffed her hands into the pink pockets of her fleece. "There I go mixing you guys up again. I guess you think I'm stupid."

Tyler shook his head. "No way. You're one of the smartest people I know."

Emma looked down at her boots. "Yeah right." Then she turned to walk away.

"No, really!" Tyler called after her. He reached out and touched her shoulder.

Emma looked back. "No need to patronize me."

"I'm not!" Tyler protested. "Look. When Sydney and I were painting sets I heard you rehearse the play. You memorized the whole thing before anyone else. That made me think of all the other times you memorized stuff."

Emma wrinkled her forehead. "Like when?"

"Like in third grade when you knew every single tall tale before the teacher told us about them. You could recite a lot of them by heart! You knew more about Johnny Appleseed than she did."

"That's only because we have one of his apple trees growing in our backyard," Emma said, blushing. "And my mom read me a book."

"Well, what about in fourth grade when you dressed up like Sacajawea for the Festival of the Famous?"

"So what?"

"You taught me more about Lewis and Clark than anyone."

"Only because Sydney helped me learn by drawing a bunch of pictures."

"Sydney wasn't there dressed up in moccasins with a doll slung on her back passing out smoked salmon. That was brilliant."

"Really?" Emma asked. "You didn't think it was silly?"

"No, Emma, it wasn't. That was being a good teacher."

"A teacher?"

"Yeah," Tyler said. "You'd be a great teacher."

"I don't know about that."

But Tyler had thought about that a lot. "What about

telling Caleb to watch a DVD to help him learn his lines for the play?" he asked. "Caleb's watched the movie so many times my whole family has *The Wizard of Oz* memorized." Tyler gently elbowed Emma in the side. "I should complain about how annoying it is."

Emma laughed. "Sorry."

"I know you're smart, Emma. So don't think I don't."

"You and Caleb look so much the same," Emma said. "And I have trouble telling 'b' and 'd' apart. So how am I supposed to know if it's you or Caleb?"

"Just ask," Tyler said. "It's no big deal."

"I'm not very good about asking for help. At least that's what Miss Klimey says."

"We all have things we could be better at."

The first bell rang, signaling the end of recess. "Yeah, um. Thanks for the pep talk," Emma said. The doors opened, and students streamed into the hall.

"Emma, wait! Is something the matter?"

But in the press of kids, Tyler's question evaporated like steam.

15
TRUTH BREAKS FREE

CALEB counted the hours. It was Friday afternoon which meant pretty soon it would be Saturday. When the following morning dawned, Caleb and Tyler would pop corn and watch the original *Star Wars* trilogy with their dad. That's what they did every year on the first day of winter vacation. Episode Four, Episode Five, and Episode Six—all the way from Luke working his uncle's moisture farm on Tatooine to the Ewoks partying at the end of *Return of the Jedi*.

By that point their mom would come home from the hospital cranky and yell at them about too much screen time. Then she'd make Caleb and Tyler go outside "to get some fresh air" and they wouldn't be able to watch Episodes One, Two, and Three until Sunday.

Mom completely misses the point that the Star Wars

marathon is the most important part of Christmas, next to presents. Caleb thought. *It's an Adler family tradition!*

But first he had to get through Mr. Baker's class. The movie with Tiny Tim was all over and now they were supposed to copy a bunch of facts off the board about Victorian England. Like that was supposed to make up for Mr. Baker letting them watch a random film that had nothing to do with anything.

Caleb's pencil was down to the nub. He didn't know who Prince Albert was, and he didn't care. He wrote down something about Queen Victoria and then snuck a peek at Sydney. She was in the corner staring out the frosty window. There was nothing remotely ninja-ish about the brown sweatshirt Sydney wore. Her hair was pulled back into a ponytail and she wore old jeans.

"Miss Silver," Mr. Baker asked, jolting Caleb back to attention. "Is there a problem?"

Caleb looked at Emma. There wasn't anything on Emma's desk but her iPad. From the corner of his eye, Caleb saw Sydney turn away from the window to watch what happened next.

"No, Mr. Baker," Emma said. "There's no problem. I'm listening."

"Then why aren't you writing anything down?" he asked.

Emma folded her hands on top of her desk and sat up straighter. "I'm giving you my full attention while you explain each fact. Then I'm going to take a picture of the board when you're done."

Mr. Baker burped. "Excuse me," he said. "The assignment, Miss Silver, is to copy this information down from the board."

"So we will learn it," Emma said. "Yes. I'm learning the information by listening and I'll also have a copy of the board on my iPad."

"What a cool idea," Tyler said. "Can I do that too?" Caleb wished he'd thought to say that. There was a chorus of agreement from the classroom.

"Of course not!" Mr. Baker glared at Emma. "Do what you need to do, but don't be disruptive."

Emma wasn't disruptive—she was the most peaceful person Caleb knew. And he thought it was lousy for Mr. Baker to make it sound like Emma was causing problems. Caleb was about to say so when Sydney stood up. One look was all it took for Caleb to know Sydney's inner-ninja was alive and well.

"Emma's doing great." Sydney pushed up the sleeves of her sweatshirt, showing wrist-to-elbow doodles.

"She's not disruptive either," said Tyler, who was also on his feet.

Caleb looked over at Emma, who was squeezing her eyes shut tight. He reached out across the aisle and put his hand on her back. Emma didn't flinch. She opened her eyes and looked at Caleb. "It's okay," Caleb whispered. He saw tears on Emma's cheeks.

"Sit down," said Mr. Baker. "Get back to work."

A snarl grew from deep inside Caleb that made him want to lunge at Mr. Baker. But his anger was checked by Emma.

"Of course, Mr. Baker," said Emma. "Thank you for understanding."

Emma's politeness worked a miracle.

Mr. Baker half smiled.

EMMA'S mom thought she and Sydney had biked to the library, but they hadn't. They were in the lobby of Cascade Brooks. *I'm not a liar,* Emma thought. *But this is too important to risk Mom saying I couldn't go.* The day before, when Sydney told Emma what was going on with Caleb and Tyler's grandma, Emma didn't know whether to call her mom, tell Miss Klimey, or just throw her arms around Sydney like a net of protection. Visiting somebody else's grandma was bizarre. Doing it in secret was even stranger.

But when Emma saw the picture of herself, or "Sonia" or whatever, drowning, Emma was intrigued. *Wasn't that what Caleb's grandma called me at the Olive Garden?* There was more to the story than she was hearing—Emma was positive. *And Sydney's on edge*, Emma thought to herself. *I need to help.*

That's why she agreed to come today. That's why she lied to her mom.

The first thing Emma noticed was the gigantic aquarium of tropical fish in the foyer. It looked out of place next to the blown-up snowman. Emma wasn't sure what she thought an old folks' home would look like, but it wasn't this. She and Sydney slathered on hand sanitizer, and headed down the hall. There was an advertisement for water aerobics posted in the elevator.

Emma shuddered. It was hard to picture old people in swimsuits. "Are you sure this is okay?" she asked Sydney for the millionth time.

"Don't worry, Emma," Sydney said, taking off her brown jacket. "Mrs. Adler expects us."

"You remember our deal, right?" Emma asked Sydney. "I'll visit Mrs. Adler if you see Dr. Victoria."

Sydney blew bangs out of her face with a hot breath. "I'll go, but I promise you, it's a waste of time."

"Maybe so. But my mom researched every last psychologist in Seattle before she selected Dr. Victoria. We want you to give her a try. Your mom really likes her."

"I don't care about my mom."

"It's not for your mom," Emma said. "It's for you. You deserve help too."

Sydney shrugged.

The girls walked down the hallways in unnatural quiet. The sterile smell reminded Emma of blue toilet water.

When they got to room 305 Sydney lifted up her fist to knock. Before she did, she looked back at Emma. "Maybe you should wait a second—over to the side. Okay?"

Emma blinked. "Sure." She slipped over a few steps. A few moments later Emma heard the door open and an old lady talking. "It's you!" the voice said. "Four o'clock on the dot. You're my most faithful student." Emma squirmed. *It was only 3:45.*

"You're my most favorite teacher," Sydney said. "But Mrs. Adler, wait. I brought a visitor. Somebody I thought you'd like to see."

"Oh?" asked Grams. "Who's that?"

Emma felt Sydney grab her arm and pull her into the doorway.

"This is my friend Emma."

Emma looked into a face with wrinkled and papery-thin skin. But something about the nose reminded her of the twins. "Hello, Mrs. Adler. Nice to meet you."

Grams was already tearing up. "Sonia," she whispered. "It's you!"

Before Emma knew what was happening she felt waspish arms encircle her, pulling her into the studio apartment.

"It's you! It's you!" Grams cried. Then she spun Emma around in a tiny little dance. "Sonia, you're here!"

Emma pulled herself away. "I'm not Sonia," she said. "I'm Emma." *This is getting weird.*

"Let's sit down," Sydney said. "I'll make the tea."

"Yes, dear," Grams said to Sydney. "Please do." Then Grams turned back to Emma, staring at her longingly. "We can sit down on the couch."

"Um, okay." Emma looked at the room. The blue walls were an attractive contrast to the green furniture. She noticed an enormous abalone shell resting on a bookcase that tied the colors together. When Emma sat on the couch, she glided her hands across the velvet.

"Sonia." Grams reached out and pulled a tendril of Emma's brown hair behind her ear. "You came back to me."

"I'm sorry, Mrs. Adler," Emma tried again. "I'm not Sonia. I'm Emma."

"No, Sonia," Grams said, dissolving into tears. "I'm sorry. I'm so sorry."

"Hey, wait!" said Sydney, coming over with mugs of tea. "Don't cry. It's all good." She sat on the other side of Grams and hugged her. "I brought my friend here so you could be happy. So you could talk to her and see her again."

Grams leaned her head on Sydney's shoulder for a moment. "Thank you, dear. Thank you so much." Then

Grams looked back at Emma. "Now I can say the things I've needed to say forever."

Emma swallowed hard.

"Yes, Mrs. Adler," Sydney said. "Exactly."

Grams took both of Emma's hands in her own. Her grip was surprisingly strong. *What did Sydney get me into?* Emma thought. But she looked Grams right in the eyes—eyes that were the same shade of blue as her own.

"Sonia, I'm sorry," Grams said. "I shouldn't have told you to get in the water. I knew you weren't as good a swimmer as I was. You especially hated the cold. And Mom told us to stay off the beach. She told us to stay out of Puget Sound. You listened, but I didn't. It wasn't your fault! It was mine." Grams cried so hard Emma could barely understand her. "It's my fault that you're gone forever."

"But she's not gone," Sydney said. "She's right here sitting with you, so you can be happy."

Grams smiled warmly. "Yes," she said, tears streaming down her face. "You're here, Sonia. You're here!"

Emma looked at Sydney, unsure what to do.

"Say something," Sydney whispered. "Say anything."

No matter what she told her mom about where she was going that afternoon, Emma wasn't a liar, but she *was* an actress.

"I'm here," she told Grams. "I'm here for you, and I love you."

Somehow, Emma thought, *that seems like the right thing to say.*

SYDNEY had triple wrapped the artwork in plastic garbage bags to protect it from the rain, but she shielded it under her raincoat anyway. She looked over at Emma holding a giant golf umbrella. It was Saturday morning and they were standing on Caleb and Tyler's front porch.

"Are you sure, Emma?"

"Yeah, Sydney. We've got to."

"But what if they don't let me see Grams anymore? What if they flip out?"

Emma sighed. "We've been over it a thousand times. You have to tell them. It's the right thing."

Sydney looked at the doorbell. "I know." She held out her finger and pressed the button.

The door swung open.

Ava stood in front of them holding a can of pop. "Hi, Sydney. Is your brother with you?"

"Um, no." Sydney clutched the artwork tighter. "Could I talk to your dad?"

"My dad?" Ava raised her eyebrows. "I guess." She held open the door.

The living room was dark except for Yoda, larger than life on the flat-screen TV. Sydney saw Tyler, Caleb, and their dad sprawled out on couches, watching *The Empire Strikes Back*.

"Is that Brian?" called out Mr. Adler. "Come join the fun."

"Wrong guess," Ava said.

The twins turned to look and then sprung up to sit. Tyler reached for the remote and pressed 'pause.'

"Sydney," Caleb sputtered. "What are you doing here?"

Sydney unzipped her raincoat and took out the plastic-wrapped art. "I need to talk to your dad." She looked at Mr. Adler. "It's important."

Mr. Adler nodded his head towards the lamp. "Sure. Could you get the lights, Tyler?"

A few minutes later all of them were sitting around the coffee table. Sydney had the unopened artwork on her lap.

"I've got a confession," she said, squeezing her hand into a fist. "I've been visiting your mom so she could give me art lessons."

"I know," said Mr. Adler.

Sydney's eyes got big. "You know? How'd you know? It was a secret!"

Mr. Adler smiled. "Cascade Brooks is a sheltered environment. They won't give my mother's room number to a stranger. The receptionist called me, the first time you came, to ask my permission."

"Why didn't you tell us?" Tyler asked his dad. "Is that why Grams started painting again? Because of Sydney?"

Mr. Adler nodded.

Sydney was stunned. "What do you mean, 'started painting again?' When did Mrs. Adler stop painting?"

"A year ago," Mr. Adler answered. "Mom had forgotten everything about art until Thanksgiving. Until she met you."

"I don't understand," said Emma. "How could Mrs. Adler forget something like that and then remember? I thought when you had Alzheimer's you only forgot."

"It comes and goes," said Caleb, quietly. "You never know when the memories will be there."

"Sometimes Grams will remember something in great detail," Tyler added, "and then other times she forgets the most basic things ever."

Sydney felt like a little part of her heart broke when she heard that. She knew Grams had issues, but she didn't know they were that bad.

"You helped my mom remember something really important to her," Mr. Adler said to Sydney. "Her art makes her happy."

Sydney wiped her nose on her sleeve. "I'm not sure if I'm making Mrs. Adler remember happy things or not." She looked at Emma.

"It's okay," Emma whispered. "Show them."

Sydney unwrapped her package and held up the picture of Sonia drowning in seaweed. "A few days ago your mom drew this."

Tyler gasped. "It's Emma!"

"Why'd Grams draw you?" Caleb demanded.

Emma slowly shook her head. "It's not me."

"No," Sydney said. "It isn't." She held up the picture Grams had drawn the day before, right before she and Emma had left. It was a portrait of two girls standing side-by-side with their arms around each other. They looked like two identical versions of Emma. "Mrs. Adler drew pictures of her twin sister Sonia."

"Grams didn't have a twin," Caleb blurted out.

"That's crazy," Ava added. "It's another memory glitch. That's all."

Tyler looked at his dad. "Tell them, Dad. Tell them it's not true."

Mr. Adler held up the picture and studied the faces. "It is true," he said softly. "All of it."

I wish it wasn't, thought Sydney. *I was still hoping.*

Tyler grabbed the picture of Sonia drowning. "Why didn't you tell us?"

"Grams had a twin and Sydney found out first?" exclaimed Caleb.

Mr. Adler slumped his shoulders. "I didn't find out myself until you two were born. My mom was so sad about Sonia drowning that she never mentioned her sister until she saw me holding both of you in my arms. Then the story spilled out. Grams made me promise not to tell you because she didn't want you growing up afraid to lose your twin like she had."

"So why'd she tell Sydney?" asked Tyler, glaring.

"Because of me," Emma answered. "Because I look so much like Sonia—and your grandma too, I guess."

"There is a remarkable resemblance," admitted Mr. Adler.

"The Olive Garden," Caleb mumbled. "She called you 'Sonia.'"

"Yes," Emma answered.

"What?" Mr. Adler asked.

"Nothing," said Caleb quickly.

Sydney looked down at the portraits. "I brought Emma to see Mrs. Adler yesterday," she said, "and your grandma was so happy to see Sonia that we didn't correct her."

"I get it." Tyler grunted. "That's what I would have done too."

Sydney couldn't help it. Tears welled up inside her that wouldn't be stopped. "She got to say goodbye," Sydney whispered. "She got to say goodbye to Sonia." Sydney felt Emma's arms wrap around her tight. Then she felt Ava hugging her too.

"She got to remember," said Mr. Adler. "Thank you."

And Sydney knew with every heartbeat that being able to say goodbye was a gift. But being able to remember was an even better one.

Then Sydney asked the tough question. The one that she was terrified of asking. "Can I still visit Mrs. Adler for art lessons?"

Mr. Adler smiled so hard the corners of his eyes crinkled. "You can visit my mom as long as she wants you to."

Sydney felt her heart practically burst open. Tears started streaming down her cheeks.

"It's okay," said Emma, patting Sydney's back. "He said 'yes.'"

"I know." Sydney sobbed. "I know."

"Then why are you crying?" Mr. Adler asked.

"Because I don't know what I would have done if you'd said 'no.'"

16

THE COWARDLY LION PUCKERS UP

CALEB peeked around the curtain into a sea of faces. The auditorium was packed. He was sweating hard, but not due to stage fright. The twins were switching places one more time because as Tyler pointed out, it was a lot easier to talk to pretty girls when you were pretending to be someone else.

Caleb released the curtain and looked over at his brother Tyler, who was wearing the lion costume. It was a plush-covered monstrosity. Caleb watched as Emma wandered up to Tyler, twisting the end of one of her Dorothy pigtails.

It's now or never, Caleb thought. He pulled his hair across his forehead and walked over to where Sydney and her mom were talking.

"I'm so proud of you, sweetie. This scenery is amazing," Mrs. Taylor gushed. "You're doing a great job as a stagehand."

Caleb saw Sydney nod at him when he approached. "I couldn't risk Tyler dropping my picture of the Emerald City," she teased.

Right then Mrs. Taylor's cellphone buzzed. "That's Brian," she said. "He's saving me a seat in the front row." Mrs. Taylor enveloped Sydney in an enormous hug. At first, Sydney let her arms dangle, but then she hugged her mom back. "We'll go out to dinner at the Space Needle, okay?" Mrs. Taylor said. "And keep talking? Like Dr. Victoria suggested?"

"Sure," Sydney answered.

Caleb watched Mrs. Taylor hurry away. Then he stared at Sydney and felt his heart beat hard.

"So, Tyler," Sydney said. "The sets *are* pretty amazing. Even the parts you did."

"Yeah," Caleb agreed, "we make a good team."

"Ten minutes to curtain!" Mr. Day called.

"Well," Sydney mumbled. "We'd better—"

But before Sydney could finish her sentence Caleb leaned forward until their faces were inches apart. "I want you to know," he said, "that I really like you."

"You do?" Sydney smiled. Then, right when Caleb was mustering up the courage to reveal his true identity, she kissed him, smack on the lips. The kiss felt warm and squishy.

"Wait!" Caleb squealed. "I'm not Tyler, I'm Caleb."

"You're Caleb?" Sydney jerked back.

"Did someone say my name?" asked a voice from the corner. Tyler walked over swishing his tail. Emma followed.

Sydney turned her head towards Tyler and then whipped it back to Caleb. She reached up and pulled Caleb's hair back from his forehead.

"Ow!" Caleb protested. "Not so hard."

"Freaking heck!" Sydney shouted. "You're—"

"In a big rush to get my costume on." Caleb answered, his armpits feeling sweaty.

"What happened?" asked Emma.

Tyler grabbed Emma's hands. "You're the smartest, bravest, kindest girl I know," he blurted out. "There, I said it." He dropped her hands and took the lion mane off. "I believe this is yours, Caleb."

"Thanks." Caleb crammed the wig on his head.

"You were in on this too, Tyler?" Sydney exploded. "You liar! You sneak! You good for nothing—"

"Ladies and gentlemen," Mr. Day hissed. "The audience can hear you."

Sydney's face was purple.

"Yup," Caleb said. "I better go change into the rest of my costume."

Sydney grabbed the back of his shirt as he turned to

go. "Caleb Adler," she said with a voice like venom. "You'd better watch out!"

And Caleb knew, with a shudder of delight, that this meant war.

THE END

AUTHOR'S NOTE

Watching a loved one progress through the stages of Alzheimer's disease is difficult, and talking about it is even harder. That's why I wrote THE GIFT OF GOODBYE. It's a story for kids, about kids, *not* about Alzheimer's disease. A book that was primarily focused on dementia would have been too sad for children to read. But I know that there are lots of kids in America right now who are witnessing Alzheimer's change their grandma or grandpa. If THE GIFT OF GOODBYE helps one reader feel less alone, then my effort was worth it.

I wrote THE GIFT OF GOODBYE in 2013 and 2014 when my grandma was still in an Assisted Living apartment at her retirement community. I had many family members read my manuscript, and all of us felt like the character of Grams was an accurate representation of

AUTHOR'S NOTE

what Alzheimer's disease could look like. At that time my grandma would often get lost or confused, but was also able to share vivid memories of childhood. She could no longer order off of a menu when we went out to a restaurant, but she could still crack jokes and participate.

But in 2018 when I prepared THE GIFT OF GOODBYE for publication, I struggled with wanting to rewrite the character of Grams. My presentation of Grams's Alzheimer's disease no longer felt authentic. How could Grams be able to remember so many things? Why had I made her so articulate? The truth was that my own grandmother has slipped so far into Alzheimer's that I no longer recognized her in Grams.

Four years from opening night of the play, this is how the story continues. Sydney still visits Grams, only they no longer do art lessons. Caleb comes too and the three of them sit on a couch in a sunny window and look at pictures from art books. Grams doesn't know who Sydney and Caleb are, but she is happy to see them.

Sydney turns the pages and points out qualities about each painting that she likes. Grams nods, and taps the pictures.

Caleb doesn't say much. He looks around the clean

AUTHOR'S NOTE

and cheery memory care unit and is glad that Grams has a safe place to live.

Tyler hasn't visited Grams in two years because it became too hard for him. It's okay that Tyler no longer comes. Grams wouldn't want him to suffer.

Emma is grateful that nobody in her family has been diagnosed with Alzheimer's disease, but she wants to support her friends. That's why, as student council president of her high school, Emma rallies people to form teams in the Walk to End Alzheimers's®.

Tyler designs t-shirts for the four of them to wear that say "TEAM GRAMS" and have a perfect rendition of a cat drinking a latte, surrounded by four kittens.

One day there will be a cure to end Alzheimer's disease, and kids like Caleb, Sydney, Emma, and Tyler will help find it.

If you want to form your own team visit: https://act.alz.org to find a Walk to End Alzheimers's® near you.

ABOUT THE AUTHOR

Louise Cypress believes in friendship, true love, and the everlasting power of books. She wrote this book because she loves her grandmother with all her heart, and is still trying to say goodbye.

Be the first to find out about Louise Cypress's next book. Sign up for The YA Gal Newsletter, managed by Louise's friend, Jennifer Bardsley.

https://landing.mailerlite.com/webforms/landing/r4g0k3

Did you enjoy THE GIFT OF GOODBYE? Pretty-please-with-a-big-bow-on-top review it on Amazon. Louise will be eternally grateful.

ALSO BY LOUISE CYPRESS

BITE ME

HUNT ME

SLAY ME

MERMAID ABOARD

BOOKS, BOYS, AND REVENGE

SNEAK PEEK OF BOOKS, BOYS, AND REVENGE

When fifteen-year-old Kayla Dexter "gets dumped" by her best friend since third grade, she reinvents herself using books, boys, and revenge.

Kayla is intense, sincere, and sincerely intense. She's thrilled to be starting tenth grade at La Jolla Prep Academy, even though she doesn't have nearly as much money as her classmates. Thankfully, Kayla's best friend Amanda Swenson helps her blend in.

But when Kayla unintentionally offends new girl Victoria Lancer, she discovers just how mean high school girls can be. Kayla's rise to YouTube stardom happens in the worst possible way. The cruelest part is that Amanda sides with Victoria.

Kayla's circumstances change for the better when she dates Logan Robinson, a junior who brings an instant group of friends with him. But a disastrous night at Winter Formal helps Kayla discover something important: the only hero she needs is herself.

So with her diary in one hand and a pocket recording device in the other, Kayla captures all of the moments that matter. Victoria better watch out! Kayla's line between justice and revenge is thin. When La Jolla Prep Academy hears what's on Kayla's computer, everyone will take notice... including Amanda.

Turn the page to start reading!

CHAPTER ONE: BOOKS, BOYS, AND REVENGE

TUESDAY, SEPTEMBER 8

Dear Diary,

It's been a pressure cooker of learning around here for years. Don't blame my mom because she's always telling me to stop being so intense, but I've been plotting to go to La Jolla Prep Academy forever. It's the best, most prestigious, most expensive private school in all of San Diego. Most people don't go to La Jolla Prep unless their parents are loaded. My family is *almost* upper middle class, but that doesn't mean we can afford the $30,000 tuition. All

CHAPTER ONE: BOOKS, BOYS, AND REVENGE

of my friends from our ninth grade mid-high were heading to La Jolla Prep but me until I aced that admissions test.

The La Jolla Lights Ladies Society thinks I'm a "needy but deserving student." They said those exact words right there on my scholarship certificate. If anyone at La Jolla Prep thinks I'm "needy," I'm done for. The whole point of high school is to blend in. That's why Amanda Swensons's the only person I told about my scholarship. I know I can trust Amanda because we've been joined at the hip since third grade.

She's the one who gave me this diary. "Just because your mom is too freaked out about the internet to let you start a blog doesn't mean you shouldn't write," she said. So here goes.

Today was the first day of tenth grade. The navy blue La Jolla Prep uniform looks smoking hot on me if I do say so myself. It's hard to go wrong with a plaid skirt, a white blouse, and a matching blazer. The only choice we get is in accessories, so I added my fake UGG boots from Payless and my BFF necklace from Amanda.

I woke up at five am to use the flat iron, and my hair was as smooth as Jessica Maxwell's. But by third period my hair frizzed up like a Shih Tzu's, so tomorrow I need to remember to bring hairspray to keep in my locker. I also need to memorize my locker combination. In the meantime, Amanda is helping me remember it.

CHAPTER ONE: BOOKS, BOYS, AND REVENGE

When I came out of fourth period and stood on the brick steps overlooking the quad, I almost lost my Pop Tarts. La Jolla Prep is huge. But then I saw Amanda, Jessica, and Rachel Baxter sitting under an oak tree in the middle of the quad eating their lunches. Just looking at my friends helped me stand up straighter. I glided down the steps to them and took my place. Amanda cleared a spot for me right next to her backpack.

"How was Spanish?" Rachel asked me as she picked ham off her sandwich. Rachel never eats meat, but her housekeeper Lupe keeps trying to change her mind. When I was over at Rachel's house this summer, I saw a magazine sticking out of her bookshelf that said: "Lose weight by being a vegetarian." I don't know if that's Rachel's plan or not. I think Rachel's fine the way she is.

"Spanish was *muy bueno*," I answered. Everyone is taking French but me. (Which is ridiculous since we live twenty minutes from the Mexican border.)

Jessica sat on the grass like she was a prima ballerina. Instead of cross-legged like the rest of us, she was reclined slightly to the side, keeping her shoulders thrown back, and her neck elongated. "French class was *très bien*. What did you think, Victoria?"

Victoria Lancer, the new girl from our carpool, adjusted her necklace. "I don't want to be mean, but Mademoiselle Marshall's accent is pathetic. For a second there I couldn't tell if she was teaching French or Italian.

CHAPTER ONE: BOOKS, BOYS, AND REVENGE

I should give her my dad's business card. He's a brain surgeon, you know. Whenever I meet someone I don't like, I give them Dad's card and say, 'Maybe you should have your head examined.'"

Jessica, Rachel, and Amanda all cracked up. I laughed too after a moment.

"Where'd your dad go to medical school?" Jessica asked Victoria.

"Harvard," Victoria answered in a superior-sounding tone.

"My dad went to Harvard too!" bragged Jessica. "Where did your dad go to college, Kayla?"

"Arizona State." As soon as I said that, Jessica rolled her eyes. I thought that was rather rude, but I didn't know what to do. "But I want to go to UCLA."

"Cool, Kayla," said Victoria. "I think you would be perfect for UCLA. The Ivy Leagues aren't for everyone."

I blinked in response. What was that supposed to mean? UCLA is an incredible school!

Luckily, Amanda came to my defense, like always. "My dad didn't go to college," she said with a smile that was directed at me. "And he turned out fine."

SUNDAY, SEPTEMBER 13

CHAPTER ONE: BOOKS, BOYS, AND REVENGE

Dear Diary,

I was completely wrong about Victoria. She's not a snob after all. Last night she invited Jessica, Rachel, and me over to her house for a sleepover. Amanda couldn't come because she had art class.

Victoria lives in a gated community, and she had to buzz us in before we could drive up the street. The security guard was a big, burly guy with a fancy uniform who sneered at Mom's Subaru. While we waited for him to call the Lancer house and ask for permission to open the gate, I broke out in a sweat and had to flap my arms around so I wouldn't have pit stains when I finally made it to Victoria's house.

"So," Victoria said, as she led us across marble floors to the kitchen, "I bet you guys have been to lots of sleepovers together since you've known each other for so long."

"Um... sort of," I said. I looked at Jessica. Sometimes I wonder if she's my friend at all. The last time we were at a sleepover together was in third grade when she'd put my hand in water.

"Yeah," said Jessica. "I can never look at a *My Little Pony* sleeping bag without thinking of Kayla." Then she grinned.

CHAPTER ONE: BOOKS, BOYS, AND REVENGE

Rachel eyed the pizza laid out on the granite. "I didn't meet up with everyone until sixth grade."

"Now I get to be the new girl," said Victoria.

After dinner, we went up to Victoria's room and listened to the new Taylor Swift album. But halfway through the second song Victoria's mom knocked on the door and said, "Victoria? Do you need a reminder?" Victoria muttered something under her breath, but then she slid off her bed and switched her iPod over to Mozart. I have no idea why her mom is so strict about music, but it's cool that Victoria has surround sound speakers.

My parents never have extra cash to burn like that. My dad's a city planner and my mom works for the newspaper. All of our money goes toward annoying things like my brother's swimming lessons or the credit card bill.

But Victoria's room looks like it came straight out of the pages of a Pottery Barn Teen catalog, complete with a queen size bed, a matching dresser, and a shag rug that coordinates with the curtains. There are pictures from France and a bunch of ticket stubs from the San Diego Opera all over her bulletin board. I also saw some red ribbons from gymnastics.

"You take gymnastics?" I asked her. Victoria and Jessica were trying on cashmere sweaters. Rachel was in the Papasan chair in the corner sitting on her hands. I think she might have been afraid that Victoria's clothes wouldn't fit her.

CHAPTER ONE: BOOKS, BOYS, AND REVENGE

"I used to take gymnastics." Victoria pulled a sweater over her head. "My mom made me quit because I'm too tall."

I looked at Victoria standing there in front of her full-length mirror. She's barely five-feet-two! But all I said was, "Bummer."

"Yeah." Victoria tied a silk scarf in her hair and considered the look. "Mom's right, though. Now I have more time for French lessons." She threw the scarf to the ground and pulled her hair into a messy ponytail instead.

"Kayla should try that one on," said Jessica. "It'll look better with blonde hair." She picked the silk scarf off the floor and handed it to me.

You know what? I don't know why everyone says sophomore year sucks because so far tenth grade is excellent. And I was wrong about Jessica. Instead of being my sometimes-friend, she's more like my backup bestie.

FRIDAY, OCTOBER 9

Dear Diary,

It's been a month since high school started and I think

CHAPTER ONE: BOOKS, BOYS, AND REVENGE

my favorite part is eating lunch with my friends under our oak tree. Jessica says that her brother Michael, who's a junior, calls our squad the "Sophomore Herd," but I don't care. The next time Michael and his water polo buddies walk past us, I'm going to "moo" in protest.

I said something about this at lunch today, and Victoria said, "Don't 'moo,' Kayla, it would be soooo embarrassing." Whatever. It doesn't matter if Michael's six feet tall now and looks like a lifeguard; Victoria doesn't know what Michael is really like. Helping me wash my sleeping bag back in third grade was probably the only decent thing he's ever done.

But the Sophomore Herd had more important things to discuss today than Michael and his asinine nickname. We all got back our progress reports, and I'm the only one getting all As! Amanda and Rachel's grades were pretty good, Victoria had straight Bs, and Jessica had a C. I didn't want anyone to feel bad, so I said, "The only reason that I'm getting an A in math is because Amanda's tutoring me."

"That, and a miracle," Amanda joked.

"Well, why aren't you helping Amanda with her English grade, Kayla?" asked Jessica. Everyone turned and looked at me. I knew I had to choose my words carefully. Every time I try to help Amanda with her essays, it's a disaster.

"But that *is* my thesis!" she'll say, even though what

CHAPTER ONE: BOOKS, BOYS, AND REVENGE

she's usually written is junk. Then, when I try to explain what's wrong, she won't listen.

"I guess I'm not a very good teacher," I answered. I saw Amanda look away.

I don't think anyone was listening to me by that point anyway because Jessica had started to cry about her C in history. Victoria hugged her and said, "Our fathers went to Harvard, so we're basically guaranteed to go there too."

That's so unfair! I'm not sure I want to go to Harvard instead of UCLA, but would I even have a chance to get in? I was thinking about this right when Michael showed up. (That's probably why I forgot to moo.) When Michael saw that his little sister was crying, he gave Jessica a big hug. Then he sat down next to us and popped open a bag of chips.

"Hey, Blondie," Michael said to me, "what happens if you look in the mirror at three in the morning and say, 'Bloody Mary' ten times in a row?"

"I don't know. What?"

"Your mother will say, 'Shut up and go back to bed.'"

Victoria, Rachel, and Amanda laughed like hyenas. Jessica and I barely cracked a smile.

"My mom never tells me to shut up," I replied. "She's not like that."

"Jeesh, Kayla, it's just a joke," said Victoria. Then she told Michael all about her family's trip to Europe last

CHAPTER ONE: BOOKS, BOYS, AND REVENGE

summer and how they'd stayed at an exclusive hotel right next to the Paris Opera House. "There was a marble restroom and a clawfoot bathtub, and I ordered fresh chocolate croissants every morning from room service," she boasted. "The president of South Korea was staying at our hotel at the same time, and I met her."

At this point in the conversation, I don't know what got into me. I guess I was tired of hearing Victoria drone on and on about how expensive her vacation was. So when she claimed that the president of South Korea invited her family out to dinner at Versailles, I said something like, "I'm so sure." It kind of slipped out.

Michael snort-laughed. "Wow, Blondie, you're pretty harsh." He winked at me and added, "And cute, too."

Victoria turned red in the face. "Nobody asked you, Kayla!"

All I could do was apologize profusely and try to take it back. I was just saying, "I didn't mean it! I'm so sorry!" for the fifth time when Michael took off for water polo practice.

It was my mom's turn to drive carpool this afternoon, and Victoria and Jessica didn't talk to me the whole ride home.

When I got home I saw a tweet from Victoria: "Fuggs should be illegal! If you can't afford the real thing, then go back to public school where you came from. #Loser." It had already been retweeted twelve times!

CHAPTER ONE: BOOKS, BOYS, AND REVENGE

At least *my* shoes didn't kill sheep.

SATURDAY, OCTOBER 10

Dear Diary,

I've tried texting Victoria about a hundred times this weekend to apologize for the "I'm so sure," comment, but she won't text me back. She even unfriended me on Facebook! I called Amanda last night freaking out.

"Cue up Netflix and get out the refrigerated cookie dough," Amanda said. "I'm coming over with my sleeping bag."

An overnight with my BFF was exactly what I needed. Mom picked up some take-and-bake pizzas for dinner so Amanda and I could gorge on our favorite, half pepperoni for me, half Hawaiian for her.

But later that evening after Amanda and I had watched four episodes in a row of a *Gilmore Girls* marathon that was only getting started, Mom made us go for a late night walk in the park to take a break from TV.

"Sorry," I mumbled to Amanda as Mom shoved us out

CHAPTER ONE: BOOKS, BOYS, AND REVENGE

the door with flashlights and the reflective vests Dad uses when he jogs.

Amanda clicked on her flashlight. "No prob. Your mom's always been weird about screen time. Any news yet on getting an iPhone?"

"Don't get me started. My dumbphone is the bane of my existence."

"But it has that cool slide-out keyboard."

"Maybe the Smithsonian will want it."

Amanda paused on the sidewalk and took out her phone. "Well, your mom can't keep *me* off of Instagram. Let's take a picture."

We posed for a selfie underneath the streetlight, and Amanda chose the perfect filter before adding it to her feed.

"Look," I said. "There's wet cement."

Amanda pocketed her phone. "We should write our names together."

"Let's do it!"

Amanda found a stick in the brush and wrote: Amanda + Kayla = BFF with a big heart around it, just like on our matching necklaces.

Then, when we were sitting there on the bench waiting for the cement to dry, Amanda looked at me sideways. "Kayla, I need to tell you something."

"What?"

"Jessica invited me to her party tomorrow night. Will

CHAPTER ONE: BOOKS, BOYS, AND REVENGE

it bother you if I go? Because I don't have to go if you don't want me to."

"Jessica's having a party? And she didn't invite me?" I bit my lip.

"Didn't you know?"

"No, but you should go without me. It's no big deal." I shrugged, like it wouldn't hurt my feelings if she went, and shoved my hands in my pocket.

"I knew you'd understand." Amanda zipped up her jacket. "After all, you went to Rachel's birthday last year even though I wasn't invited, and look how great that turned out."

"Yeah. We're all friends now."

"Friends forever." Amanda bent down to inspect our work. The concrete heart was already dry.

MONDAY, OCTOBER 12

Dear Diary,

I spent the last forty-five minutes of lunch today

CHAPTER ONE: BOOKS, BOYS, AND REVENGE

hiding in the restroom. I hid in a stall and pulled up my feet so nobody would know it was me.

That's because when the carpool picked me up this morning, nobody but Victoria's mom said "hi" to me. Amanda, Victoria, and Rachel just ignored me. I looked Amanda straight in the eyes, and she looked away. I stared at her for a few seconds trying to make her look back at me. But she didn't move! What's worse, Victoria and Amanda kept exchanging glances with each other and snickering. Jessica walks to school, or she probably would have mocked me too. I wondered what Mrs. Lancer was thinking because I thought I saw the corners of her mouth turn up a smidge. But mainly she kept her eyes on the road.

At first, I thought this was about my new haircut. When the rest of the Sophomore Herd was at Jessica's party on Saturday, I had five inches cut off my hair. Yeah, it's pretty short now, but it really thickened up. Even my little brother Steven says it looks nice.

But none of my friends said one word about it! Nobody talked to me in history or waited for me after English. Did something happen at Jessica's party?

When I arrived at the oak tree at lunch, I sat down next to Amanda, like always. She scooted away! Not only that, but Jessica, Rachel, and Victoria turned their backs on me too, completely cutting me off from the circle.

"Amanda," I whispered so nobody else would hear.

CHAPTER ONE: BOOKS, BOYS, AND REVENGE

"What's going on?" She took a swig from her water bottle and pretended like she hadn't heard me.

That's when I ran off to the restroom, crying.

Nobody followed me.

Since I've gotten home from school, I've tried calling Amanda over and over again. Her phone goes straight to voicemail.

TUESDAY, OCTOBER 13

Dear Diary,

I almost couldn't get up this morning. When I checked my Facebook page last night, the whole Sophomore Herd had unfriended me! I think I covered up my puffy eyes with makeup pretty well, but I guess I shouldn't have worn mascara.

Amanda still isn't talking to me, and neither are Jessica and Victoria. At least Rachel will talk to me a little bit (if nobody's looking). But maybe that's not true anymore after what happened today at the end of biology.

"What's going on, Rachel?" I asked as she was

CHAPTER ONE: BOOKS, BOYS, AND REVENGE

rushing to pack up her books. "Why is everyone ignoring me?"

"I don't want to get involved, Kayla." I thought Rachel might rip off the zipper to her backpack, she was in such a hurry to leave. I shouldn't be surprised. Avoiding conflict is Rachel's MO.

On the ninth grade East Coast trip last year, Rachel wouldn't share a hotel room with the rest of us. Her mom paid gobs of extra money so that Rachel could have her own suite. Jessica was peeved. But I figured that the real reason Rachel ditched us was that she didn't want anyone to see her sleeping in her headgear from the orthodontist. Rachel couldn't handle the stress.

But that still doesn't explain why Rachel wouldn't at least tell me what the heck was going on. "Why won't you be honest with me?" I asked. "I have no idea what I did wrong to deserve this!"

Rachel swung her backpack onto her shoulders in one quick move. "Honest?" she asked. "You want me to be honest with you? How about you be honest with me?"

"Huh?"

"Don't pretend to be stupid, Kayla. Did you tell Amanda that I was fat?"

"What? No! Of course not." Only really I had...sort of. Last summer when I spent the night at Rachel's house and saw the magazine article about vegetarian weight loss, I told Amanda all about it.

CHAPTER ONE: BOOKS, BOYS, AND REVENGE

"I didn't say you were fat," I said. "I told Amanda you *thought* you were fat. There's a big difference!"

"Whatever." Rachel was gone before I could say anything else. I just stood there, holding my biology book.

Since I didn't have anyone to sit with at lunch again, I walked from the restroom near the gym to the restroom near the science building to the restroom at the library and then back again. I didn't want to look like an obvious loser, so I spent approximately three minutes in each restroom before I moved to the next. I made this circuit about seven times, but I don't think anyone noticed. I hopefully looked like a typical tenth-grade girl washing her hands.

Carpool on the way home was the worst. It was like I wasn't there. Rachel was up front talking to her housekeeper Lupe (who was driving), Amanda and Victoria were in the middle of the minivan, and I was in the way back. Instead of talking out loud so I could hear, Amanda and Victoria kept texting each other over and over again and snickering.

I caught Amanda's eye at one point, but she quickly looked out the window.

What's going on? Why would Amanda stab me in the back like this?

CHAPTER ONE: BOOKS, BOYS, AND REVENGE

WEDNESDAY, OCTOBER 14

Dear Diary,

Today I cornered Amanda after history. I absolutely cornered her. Everyone was slamming lockers and swimming through the halls to their next class, but I went right up to Amanda and put my face smack in front of her. "Amanda Isabel Swenson," I said. *"What is going on?"* The bell rang right then, but Amanda didn't move. She just stared back at me with her face getting whiter and whiter until everyone was gone and the whole hallway was empty. We were both going to get tardy slips, but I didn't care.

"How could you do it, Kayla?" she muttered. "How could you tell everyone all those lies about my dad?"

"What are you talking about? What lies?"

"Don't try to deny it." Amanda's eyes filled up with tears. "You told everyone my dad was a failure!"

"What?"

"A failure! But he isn't! *My dad is not a failure!*" Amanda's voice got so loud all of a sudden, I thought a teacher would come out and shush us.

I shook my head, and my earrings rattled. "I never

CHAPTER ONE: BOOKS, BOYS, AND REVENGE

said that!" But as soon as the words came out of my mouth I remembered.

When I was at Victoria's sleepover with Jessica and Rachel, they'd been talking about how Amanda couldn't come because she was at art class. I'd said something like, "Amanda's dad is an artist too."

All the girls looked at me, Jessica especially.

"Yeah," I said. "He's an amazing artist."

"What does he paint?" asked Victoria.

"Well," I said. "He paints sunsets and pictures of their house, which is teeny-tiny but cute, and right on the beach."

Then Jessica asked, "Does he ever sell his paintings?"

At that point, I was starting to wonder. Was this a secret? Why hadn't Jessica known any of this? She'd been friends with Amanda longer than I had. So I decided to wrap things up. "Not that I know of," I said. "But he could if he wanted to."

When Amanda was standing there in front of her locker shouting at me, I didn't know what to do. I kept repeating over and over again that I hadn't said anything wrong about Mr. Swenson. But it didn't seem to help. Jessica and Victoria had her convinced that I told the whole world that Amanda's dad is a failed artist and that their house is crap. Really? How could anyone have a cheap home in La Jolla? This is the most prestigious beach community in all of California!

CHAPTER ONE: BOOKS, BOYS, AND REVENGE

But even still, this is what I said, "Amanda I am sooooo sorry! I never meant to hurt you, I swear! I had no idea your feelings would be hurt. That's the last thing I would want." I said this over and over again like I was on repeat. I tried to keep my voice quiet too because one person yelling was enough.

But it didn't matter. Amanda kept raging and raging at me. "You've cut me to pieces, Kayla! The whole school thinks my dad's a loser and that we live in a shack! You made it look like we were poor! And that's pretty ironic because—"

"Because what?"

"Nothing." She turned to look at her locker. "What do *you* know anyway?" Amanda said so quietly, I could hardly hear her. Then she spun around and looked at me again. "At least *my* dad is a somebody, Kayla. Your parents are nobodies."

I thought that was the worst of it, but I was wrong.

"I wish we had never been friends in the first place," Amanda said. "I wish I could go back to third grade and un-know you!"

All the while she was saying this, I stood there in front of her crying. "I'm sorry, I'm sorry," I kept sobbing. "I never meant to hurt you!" The old broken record again, but it didn't help. My best friend in the whole world was hurling abuse at me, and I had to stand there and take it.

Finally, Mr. Anker, our history teacher, poked his head

CHAPTER ONE: BOOKS, BOYS, AND REVENGE

into the hallway to see what was going on. Amanda stormed off before I could say anything else. That's when I ran off to the restroom. Again.

FRIDAY, OCTOBER 16

Dear Diary,

I'm not sure if I can do this. Facing high school without any friends is like a real-life nightmare. I don't know what to say, or what to do, or where to sit at lunch. It's pretty clear that I'm not welcome at our oak tree. I'm no longer a member of the Sophomore Herd.

Emily Clark texted me in the middle of history this morning and said, "All those conversations about you on Snapchat are horrid. I think it's mean of them, and I know you're not a cyberbully. No way did you send those pictures to the Headband Mafia."

What? I lost my breath staring at my dumbphone. Now people were saying I'm a bully? How did that happen? I looked across the classroom at Emily and gave a quick nod. Seeing her smile back made me bury my

CHAPTER ONE: BOOKS, BOYS, AND REVENGE

face in my textbook. I didn't want anybody to see me cry.

I've been searching and searching my brain trying to figure out how people could think I was a cyberbully, and I can't figure it out. Victoria was the one who made those "Alice in Wonderland" memes and sent them to Lisa Liao and her friends. Not me! I never called them the Headband Mafia even once.

It happened the first week of school. Victoria was watching Lisa Liao, Jordan Chen, and Sydney Wu eat lunch over by the drinking fountains. They all had matching hairstyles: shoulder-length bobs and headbands. "It's like they get their hair done at Super Clips," said Jessica.

"With a coupon," said Victoria. "I've been calling them the 'Headband Mafia' ever since fourth grade." Everyone laughed but Amanda and me.

"Did they go to La Jolla Prep Elementary with you?" I asked Victoria.

"Uh-huh," Victoria said. "I wish you guys had been there too."

So see? How could Victoria and Jessica be saying that *I'm* the one who's a cyberbully? I mean, maybe I should have said something at Victoria's sleepover when she sent Lisa, Jordan, and Sydney those memes from "Alice in Wonderland." Okay, I definitely should have spoken up at that moment. I should have said, "Victoria, how dare you

CHAPTER ONE: BOOKS, BOYS, AND REVENGE

make fun of those girls just because they like headbands? That's rude and insulting to every girl without bangs!" That's what I should have said but didn't. But it was too late now. Or was it?

Today at lunch I went up to Lisa and her friends and crouched down next to them while they were eating their sandwiches. I wasn't sitting, I wasn't standing, and I wasn't exactly sure if this was a good idea.

"Hi," I said. "I wanted to say that there are some really mean rumors floating around about me, and I hope you know that none of them are true."

"We know," said Lisa. "We've seen your dumbphone. No way could you make memes of that quality. Why are you crouching like that? Sit down already."

Jordan and Sydney nodded. So I sat down next to them by the drinking fountains and told them all about Victoria's party and how I watched her make the memes on her iPhone. I apologized for not speaking up for them at the time.

"It really hurt at the time," Lisa admitted.

"We thought about changing our look, but headbands are our thing," said Jordan.

"And if we gave up our signature style now," said Sydney as she ripped open a bag of snacks from Trader Joe's, "Then Victoria would win."

"Um …" I didn't know what to say. "That's really mature of you."

CHAPTER ONE: BOOKS, BOYS, AND REVENGE

"Besides," said Sydney, "Alice in Wonderland wore a hair ribbon, not a headband." She held out a small container of snacks. "Do you want a pretzel?"

"Thanks." I took one tiny pretzel and popped it in my mouth.

On the way home in carpool Emily texted me again: "Victoria, Amanda, and Jessica have a game going on right now to determine who can ignore you the longest."

I hope that Amanda doesn't win.

SATURDAY, OCTOBER 17

Dear Diary,

At the beginning of last week, it was as if I had been stabbed in the stomach. But today I texted every single girl I know in Honors English with a cut-and-paste paragraph that explained my side of the story. I received rude memes, but a few people texted back and said they believed me.

Then guess what? On that very last text, a miracle

CHAPTER ONE: BOOKS, BOYS, AND REVENGE

happened. Emily Clark called me back. When the phone chirped, I was so startled that I almost didn't answer.

"Emily?"

"Hi, Kayla, that was brave of you to send that text."

"Thanks."

"I already saw it as a screenshot on Snapchat being ridiculed, but I think it shows courage on your part for standing up to the Sophomore Herd."

"They're talking about me on Snapchat again?"

"They're always talking about you on Snapchat."

My dumbphone felt cold against my ear. "And they're lying about me?"

"Of course they're lying. Victoria Lancer is a well-known liar. She told everyone at our old school that I was a cheater!"

"Really?"

"Really," said Emily. "What happened?"

"I still don't know," Emily said. "Victoria and I used to be friends. At least I *thought* we were friends. We were on the same soccer team and everything. But then all of a sudden Victoria turned on me! She told our ninth grade science teacher that I cheated. For a while there, half of the kids at our old school believed her."

"That's awful!"

"Yeah," said Emily. "That's why when I heard what happened at Jessica's party I was outraged for you."

CHAPTER ONE: BOOKS, BOYS, AND REVENGE

I could feel my heart jump around in my chest like it was on steroids. "What happened at Jessica's party?"

"You mean you don't know?"

"I sort of know," I said. "But I don't know the exact details."

That's when Emily told me all about it. At Jessica's party, the primary entertainment seems to have been trashing me. Victoria told people that I said Jessica was dumb, Amanda lived in a shack, and that I was a cyber-bully. And the overriding topic? I was "obsessed with grades and thought I was smarter than everyone." Amanda did not say a word in my defense!

The only true part of that pack of lies is the part about me wanting to do well in school. Everyone already knows about that. But heck, it's not like I go around wearing a Harvard sweatshirt all the time like Victoria and Jessica.

"Kayla, are you still there?" said Emily. I nodded. Then I realized that wasn't very helpful when you were talking to someone on the phone.

"Yeah," I said. "I'm still here."

"Don't let her get to you, Kayla. Victoria doesn't care who she hurts. She only cares about herself."

After I had hung up the phone, I sat there on my daybed for a few minutes thinking. It was like I was in geometry class and had finally figured out the answer to a big equation. Maybe my problem wasn't Jessica, or Rachel, or Amanda. Maybe my problem was Victoria.

CHAPTER ONE: BOOKS, BOYS, AND REVENGE

MONDAY, OCTOBER 19

Dear Diary,

My "friends" still aren't talking to me. But at least I didn't have to hang out in the restrooms at lunch. Emily brought me with her to the tennis courts today so I could eat lunch with the rest of the girls' soccer team.

Everyone was sitting on the grass talking about their last match. The girls were all wearing navy plaid uniforms like me, but most of them had on Chucks. I hoped nobody noticed that I wore Keds.

I sat down next to Emily and took a bite out of my apple. Emily is tan and blonde and has naturally straight teeth. She plays soccer five days a week and still manages to bang out a pretty high GPA.

Right across from Emily was Lauren Higgins from PE. Lauren is a junior who should be shaving her arms. I mean her forearms, not her armpits; that's how hairy she is. Lauren glared at me the whole time I sat there. I don't know what her deal is, but she's as scary as Victoria.

CHAPTER ONE: BOOKS, BOYS, AND REVENGE

When Emily started talking about Victoria telling lies about people, I said, "I can't believe she told the whole school that you cheated!"

Then Lauren practically barked, "Who's Emily going to cheat off of?"

"Exactly!" I said. But that didn't stop Lauren from looking at me like I was scum.

Emily just looked back and forth between us and fake smiled. "We're all going to a Chargers game in a couple of weeks," Emily said. I think she was trying to keep the peace.

"That's great!" I exclaimed, even though I don't like football. I wasn't sure if Emily was inviting me along or not. But before I could figure that out, Lauren interrupted.

"So, Kayla," she said. "Do you play any sports?"

"Huh?"

Suddenly the whole soccer team was staring at me. It was so quiet, I could hear one of the girls crunch potato chips between her teeth.

"No," I answered. "I'm not very athletic."

"Do you watch sports?" Lauren asked.

"Um, sometimes." I felt my ears turn red. "If there's nothing else on tv."

Some of the girls chuckled. I think I even heard Lauren snort. So I inhaled the rest of my lunch and

CHAPTER ONE: BOOKS, BOYS, AND REVENGE

headed off to the restrooms. I didn't know where else I belonged.

WEDNESDAY, OCTOBER 28

Dear Diary,

In the carpool today, I kept trying not to stare at Victoria, even though she obviously wanted to get my attention. She's having everyone but me over to her house for Halloween, and that's all she talked about the whole time.

"My Halloween party is going to be a rager," she told Amanda and Rachel. "My parents said I could invite thirty people." Then Victoria looked straight at me. "I love spending time with my friends."

I almost started crying right then and there. I had to sniff hard to suck back the snot. But you know what? Victoria's mousy brown hair and tiny little nose remind me of a hamster. That's what stopped the tears.

So when Ms. Dasher had us write a Halloween-

CHAPTER ONE: BOOKS, BOYS, AND REVENGE

themed poem today in Honors English, this is what I submitted:

> **A Halloween Themed Poem** by Kayla Dexter
> Witch
> I want to call you that to your face
> but I don't dare.
> you think you are God's gift to culture
> but culture to you
> means overpriced shoes
> ugly curtains
> And pretending to speak French.

SATURDAY, OCTOBER 31

Dear Diary,

Mom just told me that Uncle Luke has lung cancer and emphysema. How's that for a miserable Halloween?

CHAPTER ONE: BOOKS, BOYS, AND REVENGE

He's had it for a while, but nobody's bothered to tell me until now.

I feel like I could punch something.

Technically, Uncle Luke's my great-uncle. He's always been my favorite, though, because he brings me a new book each time he comes over for dinner. I still have the copy of *Little Women* he gave me when I was nine.

But Uncle Luke hasn't been over to our house for a while. Mom says that Uncle Luke has been "in a funk" ever since he got his diagnosis. He spends all of his time reading books and hanging out in his garden smoking.

We went to visit Uncle Luke tonight and brought him ice cream from Dairy Queen. Blizzards are his favorite, like mine. We sat there eating on the deck in his backyard, and birds were flying everywhere because he has about a million feeders. There were so many hummingbirds zooming around, I thought I might get dive bombed. My little brother Steven kept trying to throw rocks at them.

"Settle down!" Mom screeched at Steven, which caused all the birds to fly away.

Uncle Luke pretended not to notice. "How's school going?" he asked me.

"Great," I mumbled.

"Kayla's on her way to making the honor roll," bragged Dad, "just like you, Uncle Luke."

I knew that Uncle Luke was smart like me, but I didn't

CHAPTER ONE: BOOKS, BOYS, AND REVENGE

know that he had been on the honor roll. "Did you ever think about going to UCLA?" I asked him.

"Oh, no." Uncle Luke leaned back in his chair. "I came home from Vietnam and went straight to a factory job on the San Diego docks."

"He's not telling the full story," said Dad. "Uncle Luke worked all day and put himself through college at night school. He was the first person in our family to go to college."

That's when Uncle Luke changed the subject.

"Poetry," Uncle Luke told me. "Poetry and good books can get you through anything."

I nodded my head in agreement like I knew what the heck he was talking about.

Click here to read the rest!

Made in the USA
San Bernardino, CA
21 December 2018